BRUTE FORCE
+PLUNDER

BOSTON REVIEW

Publisher & Coeditor-in-Chief Deborah Chasman

Coeditor-in-Chief Joshua Cohen

Executive Editor Matt Lord

Associate Editor Cameron Avery

Contributing Editors Thomas Ferguson, Adom Getachew, Jake Grumbach, Lily Hu, Robin D. G. Kelley, Becca Rothfeld, & Simon Torracinta

Editorial Assistant Juliana George

Production Assistant Harrison Knight

Columnists Olúfẹ́mi O. Táíwò, David Austin Walsh

Associate Publisher Jasmine Parmley

Finance Manager Anthony DeMusis III

Board of Advisors Derek Schrier (Chair), Margo Beth Fleming, Archon Fung, Deborah Fung, Larry Kramer, Richard M. Locke, Jeff Mayersohn, Scott Nielsen, Robert Pollin, Rob Reich, Hiram Samel, Kim Malone Scott, Brandon M. Terry, & Michael Voss

Print and Cover Design Rest Design

Cover Art Edel Rodriguez

Brute Force and Plunder is *Boston Review* issue 2026.1 (Forum 37 / 51.1 under former designation system).

"The War No One Wanted" is adapted from *The Return* by Salih Basheer, published in February 2026.

Supported in part by generous grants from the Open Society Foundations and the William and Flora Hewlett Foundation.

Printed and bound in the United States by Sheridan.

Distributed by Haymarket Books (www.haymarketbooks.org) to the trade in the U.S. through Consortium Book Sales and Distribution (www.cbsd.com) and internationally through Ingram Publisher Services International (www.ingramcontent.com).

To become a member, visit bostonreview.net/memberships.

For questions about donations and major gifts, contact Jasmine Parmley at jasmine@bostonreview.net.

For questions about memberships, email members@bostonreview.net.

Boston Review
PO Box 390568
Cambridge, MA 02139

ISSN: 0734-2306 / ISBN: 979-8-99374941-9

CONTENTS | WINTER 2026

S TEVE BANNON NAMED the tactic in 2018: "flood the zone." Since resuming office last January, Trump has doubled down on the maneuver, unleashing a campaign of rapid-fire destruction on immigrants, the federal government, Latin America, and beyond. The scale of the damage is staggering and growing. This issue looks at the violent reconfiguration of U.S. politics and power and what it means for democracy and resistance.

We open with Olúfẹ́mi Táíwò's column on MAGA's "vice signaling"—the shameless celebration of transgression. Unlike virtue signaling, which indicates allegiance with group values, vice signaling aims simply to own the opposition. It thus renders "the moral commitments of the in-group . . . irrelevant," eliminating any "practical constraint on anyone's behavior." This impunity plays out today in brutal displays of force that shock the conscience of most Americans.

Several other essays illuminate Trump's goal: not only to dominate but to coerce, humiliate, and silence. A special section focuses on the lethal and symbolic power of Immigration and Customs Enforcement: how violence pervades even the language of asylum hearings (Joshua Craze), how raids on Canal Street threatened both spectacular and anonymous force (Liv Veazey), and how the murders of Renee Good and Alex Pretti reflect terror tactics long deployed by U.S. police (Robin D. G. Kelley).

Tracking raw power in global affairs, Aslı Bâli and Aziz Rana trace the origins of the "Trump Doctrine" through years of U.S. lawlessness in the Middle East. Now the coercion has reached its purest form, casting aside any pretense of international law, alliances, and limits. The effect is to signal that what little sovereignty less-powerful states might have had is now openly conditional on the whims of the United States and its "civilizational superiority." The "peace" plan in Gaza exemplifies this new old imperialism, Bâli and Rana explain: it "doubles down on American presumptions that force can substitute for legitimacy and that the weak will suffer what they must."

Of course, from ICE terror in Minneapolis to regime change in Venezuela, the goal is not just an accumulation of power but the further enrichment of elites, whether through lucrative government contracts or the broader massive transfer of wealth and security away from the rest of us. Gerald Epstein unpacks crypto's designs on the global financial system, while Marie Gottschalk documents the financial entanglement of local jails with the federal deportation machine.

How do you successfully resist the shameless exercise of brute force and power? Can we avert what Vivian Gornick calls the "capitulation and inertia"—the daily accommodation of the rise of authoritarianism? Reading a memoir of a childhood in Nazi Germany, she warns that even those with moral commitments may struggle to act.

But action is essential, from anti-ICE mobilization to electoral politics. David Austin Walsh examines the promise of Zohran Mamdani's experiment in New York. Meanwhile, the fierce resistance of the people of Minneapolis has forced a national reckoning. For the Democratic Party, massive protests have challenged the decades-old conviction that moderation is the way to win and govern. Against demands to dismantle ICE, Democrats finally acted to block a DHS funding bill. But as of this writing in early February, they are poised to settle for far less: what Senator Tim Kaine insists are "reasonable" checks on ICE. Drawing lessons from movements that have reversed democratic backsliding abroad, Adam Bonica and Jake Grumbach argue that Democrats' poll-tested timidity is precisely the wrong way to defeat authoritarianism. Their bracing call for change within the party opens a large debate, with fifteen responses you can read on our website.

Finally, the archive feature in this issue brings our fiftieth anniversary year to a close. We want to express our deepest gratitude to all those who have read, shared, and supported our work as we move forward together. **BR**

Donald Trump and Secretary of Homeland Security Kristi Noem speak to reporters in Florida in July 2025. Image: Getty Images

EMPIRE OF VICE

Olúfẹ́mi O. Táíwò

CONGRESSWOMAN AND MAGA ACOLYTE turned antagonist Marjorie Taylor Greene let something revealing slip in a recent interview with the *New York Times*: "Our side has been trained by Donald Trump to never apologize and to never admit when you're wrong."

The Trump administration has indeed been marked by a combination of shamelessness and intransigence that is perhaps just as well likened to the public relations strategies of mafiosos as to those of politicians. But taken at face value, Greene's statement says more than this. It's one thing to point out that Trump and his lackeys defy norms of common decency and accountability. It's another to claim that they are spreading these habits and threatening to establish them as a new normal in American politics. And I suspect that claim is right: the Trump administration really *is* training American elites and its broader political culture as a whole.

It's not that Trump outright tells people to cultivate shamelessness. He's not exactly a life coach—beyond *The Art of the Deal*, Trump's never been much of one for communicating explicit principles. Which isn't to say he's above explicitness: as chronicled in a biopic about Trump, the admonition that "no matter what happens, you claim victory and never admit defeat" was among the rules Trump himself learned as dark apprentice to the late lawyer and fixer Roy Cohn. But lack of open acknowledgment notwithstanding, the sense in which Trump has actively "trained" Greene's side of politics is not especially subtle.

Vice signals are not just cultural messages or aesthetic poses. They also come with a body count.

The president spent Christmas Day posting on Truth Social about "Radical Left Scum" and launching missile strikes in Nigeria as a "Christmas present." If legacy media failed to dwell on these moments, it is likely in part because Trump has seldom deviated from the script of insults toward his opponents and disregard for the worth of other people's lives. What's new? Trump's open cruelty toward the tragically murdered Reiner family was less surprising than some Republicans' opposition to it—given the open hostility of many of the aforementioned toward the no less tragic attacks on Minnesota House Democrat Melissa Hortman, State Senator John Hoffman, and their spouses.

These statements and actions *are* the training. There has been much discussion in recent years about the supposed scourge of "virtue signaling," the accusation that someone has made a virtuous-seeming public statement or acted in the service of their own social standing rather than for whatever good their act might really be worth. But we could stand to spend more time discussing a related and increasingly pervasive phenomenon: vice signaling. A candid photograph that went viral on social media paints the picture vividly—Trump, Florida Governor Ron

DeSantis, and Homeland Security Secretary Kristi Noem laughing in front of the "Alligator Alcatraz" detention center hastily built to advance the administration's mass deportation campaign. The casual aesthetic of cruelty is the point. It's a way of giving viewers permission. It says, *we know what kind of person would find this monstrous: watch us laugh it up anyway to own the libs*. This is vice signaling par excellence.

At first glance, virtue signaling and vice signaling might appear to be opposites, with virtue signalers associated with do-gooders and vice signaling with more cartoonish villainy. And indeed, vice signaling is related to cruelty, schadenfreude, and evil generally. A virtue signaler is trying to look good and a vice signaler is trying to look bad—but not to *everyone*. A vice signaler typically violates moral or other standards of an out-group precisely in order to look good to the fellow members of some in-group. Vice signaling, then, is typically a version of virtue signaling rather than an alternative to it.

But there's an important catch. When we virtue signal, we are appealing to our tribe's own values, however shallow or hypocritical such appeals might be: it is the fact that our in-group treats supporting this charity or using those pronouns as a demonstration of kindness and respect that allows one to try to gain clout by adhering to the rules despite having less savory motivations in one's secret heart. But when one vice signals, the out-group's values take center stage—in order to be shirked rather than lived up to. The moral commitments of the in-group are basically irrelevant: all that matters is owning the enemy, in Trump's case the libs. And the more one relies on vice signaling as a style of action and communication, the less relevant and powerful the in-group's moral compass is as a practical constraint on anyone's behavior.

The case is pretty good that we are seeing this play out in U.S. politics writ large today. Part of Trump's initial sales pitch to voters was that "America First" meant avoiding foreign interventions and entanglements. The claim was always pretty easy to see through, but following the Christmas Day strikes in Nigeria, the abduction of a foreign leader in Venezuela, and renewed calls for the colonization of Greenland, the idea that Trump is a foreign policy "dove" might finally be a dead letter. Years ago, the idea of "states' rights" was supposedly making a revival as GOP governors engaged in open defiance of the federal government under President Joe Biden. Last year, one of these revolting governors, Greg

Abbott, volunteered his own state's National Guard to help curtail the rights of other states in service of Trump's broader attempt to fashion a makeshift federal police force. All this is to say nothing of the ongoing saga of child trafficking and assault lurking behind the Epstein files, representing exactly the kind of elite swamp Trump promised to drain.

Performative cruelty may have started with the Trump administration, but it did not and will not end there.

There's more here than garden-variety opportunism and hypocrisy. Whether or not the individual actors are being hypocritical can't explain the tepid condemnation and resistance from the rest of the party. The sheer brazenness with which the administration defies norms of truth-telling and decency is a clear message about what matters—crushing the administration's personal opponents—and an equally clear message about what doesn't: anything else, including whatever values, principles, or ideals that Trump or his party claim to stand for.

As these examples demonstrate, vice signals are not *just* cultural messages or aesthetic poses. The anonymous banker who wanted to say "retard" and "pussy" in mixed company wants to live in the world that caters to the kind of person who likes saying those words—which is why he experienced that permissiveness as feeling "liberated." The especially online members of the administration may be in it for the "ReTruths" and comment numbers in response to public chronicles of their various misadventures, but these messages also come with body counts: at least 115 in the various murders throughout the Caribbean and Pacific; at least 40 in the attack on Venezuela that culminated in the abduction of President Nicolás Maduro; and a still unknown number in the Nigeria bombings.

These strikes are completely unintelligible as tactical maneuvers: the drug-trafficking routes supposedly targeted by the military strikes have little or nothing to do with drug use in the United States; the oil reserves in Venezuela are on the other side of a multibillion-dollar infrastructure investment that U.S. oil giants have thus far demonstrated little appetite for; and Nigeria's own government officials directly contradict the White House narrative about the strike on its borders, despite collaborating with the operation itself. But all of these nevertheless make grim sense interpreted as political actions taken primarily for the sake of vice signaling and raw power projection: communicating a certain aesthetic posture to the MAGA base and its various ideological co-conspirators, training us all to allow it, and threatening all those who might disobey with the specter that the bombs will come for them next. The message says, *I can do what I want, when I want, for whatever reason I want, and you have to take it.*

Unlike complex strategic objectives that involve prioritizing and maintaining strong diplomatic relations, the thrill of vice signaling—and the training—is heightened by saying the quiet part out loud. That is exactly what Stephen Miller, now White House deputy chief of staff, did on CNN in January. "We live in a world in which you can talk all you want about international niceties and everything else, but we live in a world, in the real world," he told Jake Tapper, "that is governed by strength, that is governed by force, that is governed by power."

WE HAVE AN elite impunity problem—a global one, with the United States the worst and leading offender. As Robert Reich reminds us, twenty years ago the United States invaded a country on pretenses now widely acknowledged to be basically fraudulent. This fact barely merits an "oops" from the many actors, elected and otherwise, who promoted it—most of all George W. Bush, watercoloring into the sunset to this day. More recently, the richest man in the world helped lead mass firings of federal workers.

Meanwhile, state agents regularly kidnap immigrants and detain citizens alike in ways that are blatantly illegal. In its statement responding to the murder of Renee Good by an ICE agent in Minneapolis—caught on video and attested to by eyewitnesses, less than a mile from the site of George Floyd's own murder by a Minneapolis police officer—the Department of Homeland Security makes a set of bald-faced lies. Negative consequences for any of the aforementioned are few and far between. In the United States, political power has long meant never having to say you're sorry.

It may have started with Greene's side of the aisle, but it did not and will not end there. Michelle Obama's advice for her side of politics—to "go high" when "they go low"—has sounded more and more quaint with every passing year (a perspective she recently attempted to clarify as a call for the decidedly more combative-sounding goal of "finding purpose in your rage"). In response, upstarts like California Governor Gavin Newsom have pinned their hopes on beating Trump and the GOP at their own game, doubling down on a communications strategy of trolling and insults that Steve Bannon praised as an "energized" response to the way Trump "has changed modern politics."

It is probably no coincidence that Newsom gravitated to this strategy, having demonstrated his own taste for performative cruelty through personally helping to destroy homeless people's belongings. Moreover, if the chilling case of the British Labour Party's embrace of open hostility to immigration and immigrants is any indication, we should not expect different results from center-left parties especially when the center-left copies the right in designating the egalitarian, pro-immigration segments of its own base as the out-group to flout the moral standards of. Far more promising is the course charted out by Zohran Mamdani: one that does not shy away from conflict, but does not shy away from virtue either. Vices are best left for the vicious. **BR**

A BLIND EYE

Vivian Gornick

SOMETIME IN THE MID-1970S, I spent an evening in conversation with Mr. Sperber—a Jewish-Polish émigré I never knew by any other name—in his housing project apartment in lower Manhattan. At midnight Mr. Sperber offered to see me into a taxi, as there'd been a number of holdups recently in the project. We were alone in the elevator going down when suddenly it stopped at a floor halfway to the lobby; the door opened and there stood a teenaged Black boy. Before I could think I lunged for the "close" button. Mr. Sperber, however, held back the door, and invited the startled boy into the elevator but he, the boy, had seen my gesture and his face hardened. "Never mind," he muttered. "I'll take the next one." When the elevator door closed and I stood there, numb with mortification, Mr. Sperber turned to me and, very gently, said, "One must remain human until the last moment."

Journalist and historian Joachim Fest's *Not I: Memoirs of a German Childhood*, first published in German in 2006 and published in English in 2012 before being reissued last year, is about remaining human until the last moment.

FEST WAS BORN in Berlin in 1926, the son of a conservative Roman Catholic schoolteacher whose upright Christian morality made him a staunch anti-Nazi from the moment the first Brownshirt appeared on the city streets. Needless to say, the whole family, wife and five children, stood behind this imposing paterfamilias; as a result of their open opposition to the Nazi party, the father lost his job, the children were threatened in school, the neighbors began to shun them. The Fests lived on as the Nazi party rose to power, in poverty and isolation, but essentially untouched for a remarkably long time. Then the war caught up with them.

After managing to evade enlistment in the Hitler Youth, the Fest boys were eventually compelled to join. At the age of eighteen, unable to evade conscription, Joachim joined the Wehrmacht in order to escape being drafted into the SS. Within the year, he was captured by the Americans, spending two years as a prisoner of war. As for the rest of the family, Joachim's elder brother, Wolfgang, died on the Eastern Front and their father, Johannes, spent many months imprisoned by the Russians. Though not explicit, the implication in some of the writing is that Joachim's mother and two sisters may have been sexually abused during the Allied occupation of Berlin (for which read: by the Russians). Thus, the entire family was penalized, first as minority anti-Nazis and then as defeated Germans.

Of Hitler, Fest wrote, "He was never only their leader; he was always their voice. . . . the people, as if electrified, recognized themselves in him."

At war's end the Fests regrouped, although never again would they function as a single entity. Joachim himself became a radio journalist in the American sector of Berlin, and over the next fifteen years achieved success as a writer and editor in German radio and television. In 1973, with the publication of a major biography of Hitler, he established himself as a respected if controversial historian of the Nazi era: at a time when it was not yet popular to analyze the Nazi years in quite this way, Fest argued that the party's rise was due to millions of ordinary Germans turning a blind eye, day by day by day, to the gradual destruction of democratic law, thereby allowing the barbarism in their own hearts to manifest itself incrementally. Of Hitler himself, Fest wrote, "He was never only their leader, he was always their voice. . . . the people, as if electrified, recognized themselves in him."

Following his famed biography of Hitler, Fest wrote other books about the Nazi years, including one about the architect Albert Speer, a top Nazi minister. (In 1969, Fest had served as an editorial aide on Speer's memoirs, allowing his critics to complain that he was helping Speer dodge responsibility for the full extent of his role in the party.) At the same time, he was gaining a reputation for editorial excellence, which earned him a position as co-editor of the *Frankfurter Allgemeine Zeitung*, a renowned institution in German newspaper publishing; here he served for the twenty years between 1973 and 1993. It was only toward the end of his life that he chose to write a memoir about his family and the war. Days before the publication of *Not I*, Fest died.

FEST'S FATHER, JOHANNES, urged upon his children the avoidance of self-pity and the cultivation of irony: this latter quality, the younger Fest recalls his father telling him often, was "'the entry ticket to humanity. Outwardly one displays a seriousness the situation demands, but inwardly one snaps one's fingers at the frustrations.'" Yet it seems that Joachim, much as he loved and admired his father—and this he did inordinately—nonetheless forgot at least part of the elder Fest's admonition. While *Not I* is certainly free of self-pity, it is surprisingly straightforward both in tone and point of view, and thus entirely free of irony. The grave, even-handed calm that pervades his prose is particularly striking, sounding as though its author is intent on respecting the memoir-writing conventions of the late nineteenth century rather than those of the early twenty-first—a tone that is both the book's strength and limitation. One appreciates the calm but is put off by the emotional distance. For instance, the father loses his job and Fest writes: "Of course our meals became more modest. There were no toys anymore and Wolfgang did not get his . . . model racing car or I the football." Hardly another word on the subject. In a sense, the reader is left hanging: What was the *real* cost to the family? How did it manifest itself on a daily basis? And where is the mother in all this?

Later in the book, when a friend of the family jokingly says the Jews shouldn't leave because that was exactly what the Nazis wanted, Fest makes no comment. As for the Jews in general, the brevity of Fest's reference to them is also surprising. Everyone sees that life for the Jews is gradually shutting down. Take their neighbor and good friend, Dr. Meyer: one day he can no longer subscribe to newspapers and magazines; another, he has to hand in his bicycle and typewriter; another, he can no longer keep a pet or buy flowers. Then all the Jews simply start disappearing from the neighborhood. On a winter walk with his sons, Johannes tells the boys that someone he knows heard on the BBC that "the Jews removed from Germany were not, as was whispered furtively here and there, dumped in open country, which would have been bad enough, but were murdered by the tens of thousands." They simply could not believe that even Hitler's gangsters were capable of such monstrosity. And that's pretty much it for the Jews in *Not I*.

A great deal of attention is paid to the fact that the family, and especially Joachim, was devoted to music and literature—so much so that *Not I* often sounds like a wholesome family memoir about middle-class life in times of peace. Repeatedly and at detailed length Fest tells us what he is reading or listening to at any given moment while the war is going on: a radio broadcast of *Figaro* is transformative; absorption in the work of Friedrich Schiller is crucial; he's fallen in love with the Italian Renaissance and thinks of making it his life's work. When he's around fourteen and about to read *Buddenbrooks*, Dr. Meyer, with whom he regularly talks literature, tells him that "hardly anything in life was comparable to the pleasure of reading a book like that for the first time."

One can well believe that people as intensely middle-class as the Fests were, and such profound believers in the unassailable superiority of German civility, had "lost their instinct for danger." Johannes himself said that he "'would never understand . . . why everyone who opposed Hitler was inevitably, sooner or later, left out in the cold.'" He had thought such things "might occur in darkest Russia or the Balkans, but surely not in their law-abiding country. What had happened? That was the question raised on all sides, but no one had an answer."

Very mildly indeed, the younger Fest proffers his own: "When, toward the end of the Hitler years, they regained their senses," so many shabby compromises and betrayals had been made or committed that "it was too late."

WHILE READING *NOT I*, I could not help comparing its tale of the rise of an authoritarian regime with our situation here in America at this moment. It's not that I think we're headed for a homegrown version of Nazi Germany—I do not—but so much that is described in Fest's book feels eerily similar to what is happening right now in the United States: people being grabbed off the streets and deported, universities and law firms punished if they don't conform to an administrative ideology, federal employees fired overnight in the thousands, independent agencies abolished outright, Congress failing to assert its rights and obligations, judges being sidelined. Never in a million years could I have imagined the day when an American president would ignore a court order—and the Supreme Court would uphold his right to do so!

It's the inertia—the daily accommodation to the rise of an authoritarian regime—that is most shocking.

From one day to the next, what we in America have always thought of as law-abiding normal is disintegrating. There is not yet systematic murder of political enemies or death camps, but who knows? Whatever holds today is not guaranteed to hold tomorrow. On the other hand, perhaps it never was. Many people have re-read American law and history and found in it not only numerous loopholes but designs that, from the beginning, may have provided for the rise of dictatorial power.

More important, I think, is the incredible capitulation that seems to have taken hold in the entire country. Capitulation and inertia. It's the inertia—the daily accommodation to the rise of an authoritarian regime—that is most shocking. We—that is, Americans—live most of the time inside the cocoon of our small daily lives. Except for fire, flood, or outright war, the history-making world hardly ever impinges on most of us. For the most part, it is over there and we are over here. I watch myself and I see the divide operating clearly.

On an ordinary day, throughout most of my New York middle-class life, I wake up in the morning, check my email and flip through the pages of the *Times*—a plane crash in Maine, riots in Iran, giant pandas in a Tokyo zoo—then I eat breakfast and figure out a day that will include working at my desk, reading in the afternoon, and meeting a friend for dinner. What I have read in the *Times* makes me gasp or shudder or smile for five or ten minutes but does not seriously affect my plans for my Mrs. Dalloway day. The history-making world is still over there, and I clearly still over here.

Since Donald Trump took office one year ago, this routine has changed to the degree that I wake up, read the *Times* and, first thing in the morning, a drop of dread falls on my heart. Another piece of normalcy has just been outraged; democratic law is going down the drain; ordinary lives are upended; we're going to bomb someone who'll bomb us back. A haze of gloom begins to gather in the air around me; anxiety injects itself into the gloom. The hours pass. I think, "This can't go on! Something has to happen." Yes, there are flashes of fierce resistance, especially to the ICE raids taking place across the country, but still I can't help feeling that *nobody does anything*—not me, not the Congress, not anyone I know. And the day goes on. The news in that morning's *Times* steadily loses strength as I go about my business and lo and behold, the sky doesn't fall.

After all, the reality for many of us is that no one we know is being deported. We're not made frantic if the price of eggs goes through the roof, or the rents in Queens are beyond the beyond. By the end of the day our anxiety is what can only be called "normalized." We go to bed and wake up into another morning in which another piece of threatening news fills the front page of the *Times* and instead of being galvanized, we will merely prepare ourselves to absorb the shock.

Read *Not I* and you'll see how easily it can all happen—how easily we can all become good Germans. **BR**

ON ICE

Joshua Craze

Liv Veazey

Robin D. G. Kelley

POOR HISTORIANS

Joshua Craze

I HAD BEEN STARING at his medical records for a couple of hours, reminding myself of the details of the case. Back in 2021, I wrote a "County of Origin Expert Affidavit" for a man in Immigration and Customs Enforcement (ICE) detention I'll call Chuol (I'm using a pseudonym to protect his privacy). For such statements, I'm supposed to lean on my years of experience doing research in Sudan and South Sudan—since 2010 I've conducted extensive fieldwork in the Horn of Africa—to render an opinion on the likely consequences of someone being deported to one or the other country. Chuol was born in 1987, at the peak of Sudan's second civil war (1983–2005), in what is now South Sudan, rendering him vulnerable to deportation to both states. As a child, he fled to Ethiopia, where he spent almost a decade in a refugee camp before being resettled in Virginia in 2009.

His case file was confusing. Chuol wrote that as a child, he was conscripted into a Christian militia, though no such organization has ever existed in Sudan. It wasn't clear whether his father was killed in 1991 or 1996, or if Chuol was captured by the Sudanese government in 2000 or 2002. His story was full of holes, and the more he explained, the more confused I became. This was perhaps to be expected: Chuol had a long history of psychiatric trouble, and it is understandable that a severely mentally ill man would only have a minimal grasp of events that had occurred when he was a child. His medical records stated that he had trouble remembering things accurately. A doctor's note pondered whether he had "intellectual disabilities" and accused him of being a "poor historian." If you read his testimony with sympathy, however, you can glimpse a reality broken into pieces by poverty and violence, and marked by the absences that trauma leaves. The holes are the story. That didn't stop government lawyers from arguing that his case should be thrown out. For Department of Homeland Security (DHS) staffers looking for evidence of fraud, all the contradictions and messiness of life are invitations to a deportation.

In 2021 Chuol's case never made it to court, after ICE released him from detention for reasons I never quite grasped. Three years on, he found himself back in prison, facing deportation once again. I was preparing to testify in his case. The situation in the Sudans had not improved. A civil war had begun in Sudan in 2023 that had devastated the country, turning it into the world's worst humanitarian crisis. Just before he left office, Biden declared a genocide had occurred in Darfur. People of southern Sudanese origin were being executed, their bodies left in mass graves. In South Sudan, a government counterinsurgency was blowing up hospitals and massacring civilians. Neither country would be a viable home for Chuol.

For DHS staffers, all the contradictions and messiness of life are invitations to a deportation.

Not that America had been much of a refuge since he arrived in 2009. Chuol only had a minimal command of English, and had never really held down a job. He had spent long periods being homeless, and had accumulated a litany of crimes, principally theft and resisting arrest. His "A-file," the legal document containing his immigration history, charts, in the clinical language of the state, his descent into addiction and mental illness. His rap sheet meant that he would no longer be eligible for a renewed asylum claim, which is disbarred to all those convicted of serious crimes, no matter the situation in their country of origin. His last hope of remaining in America was what is known as a "Deferral of Removal" under the Convention Against Torture. It's a high bar. To get a DCAT ruling, as they are called, a lawyer has to show that it is more likely than not someone will face torture if they are deported, and that such torture has the acquiescence or sanction of a public official. This is precisely what was likely to happen to Chuol: the U.S. State Department and the UN have found that torture in detention by the security services of both countries is ubiquitous, a fact I hoped to make clear in my testimony. But even if Chuol got DCAT, his deportation would simply be deferred, and the matter could be re-opened at any time.

I used to get a couple of DCAT files a year, but since Trump slouched into office last January, my caseload has gone up asymptotically. None of the refugees whose cases I work on have actually fled the region's wars, despite Sudan's status as the world's worst displacement crisis. Would that these refugees could reach the United States: the U.S. resettlement program was cancelled at the beginning of Trump's term and Europe has hired militias to block refugees from coming north. Those that flee Sudan tend to be warehoused in camps in the Horn of Africa. The people whose cases I've been working on all came to the United States as children in the '80s and '90s, when the country's refugee policy was more open and its concern for the Sudanese people more deeply felt.

All these refugees have a similar story. After arriving in America, they fell between the cracks, careening between halfway houses and prisons, desperately looking for something onto which they could hold. To read their files and speak to them over bad phone lines from state prisons is to encounter fractured homes, failed schools, and fingers lost to frostbite while drunk in Minnesota. One refugee was found ineligible for asylum due to a "serious crime"—in this case, assaulting an ICE officer by spitting on him as he tried to arrest her, while she was strapped to a gurney having a psychotic episode. None of these people understand anything about Sudan's wars, which are as incomprehensible to them as to their white suburban counterparts. The only thing people like Chuol know is the name of their own ethnic group—the very fact that, in the countries to which they may be deported, will put their lives in danger.

DESPITE THE PARLOUS SITUATION in the Horn of Africa, I hadn't been successful in convincing the courts that people should not be deported to countries like Sudan, where the American government had already acknowledged a genocide was occurring. Being tortured or raped on account of your ethnic or racial background proved impossible for immigration judges in Denver or Phoenix to fathom. The centrality of Big Pharma to American life, though, turned out to offer us unexpected assistance. Most of the people for whom I wrote affidavits were severely mentally ill, and had long lists of prescription medicines accompanying their diagnoses. Neither Sudan nor South Sudan had any means of providing care for those with psychiatric problems, and neither country imported any of the drugs relied upon by the refugees I was trying to assist. In the burned remnants of hospitals in El Fasher and Old Fangak there is no Tylenol, let alone Sertraline, Risperidone, or Mirtazapine. The lawyers for those threatened with deportation used my affidavits to argue that to be deprived of one's God-given American right to antidepressants was itself a form of torture. To my astonishment, this argument convinced judges. We won, and won again, and kept winning. If imagining racialized violence abroad was beyond the US immigration system, the iniquities of the country's health care meant that judges could at least empathize with being deprived of drugs, and to such an extent that this deprivation could be the basis for DCAT decisions. I hoped we could obtain such a ruling for Chuol.

I'd been asked to testify in his deportation proceedings back in October 2024, but the case had kept getting rescheduled, leaving Chuol languishing in jail. It was June 2025 by the time his file finally came to the docket, and I was in Watamu, Kenya, a quiet town on the Indian Ocean. Reading over Chuol's medical records, I was struck by his obsession with white meat. In note after note, Chuol demanded chicken. "When you're let me get the chicken please medice," one entry read. His repeated demands would have been inexplicable if not for a later note in which Chuol told his doctors that he vomits when he eats anything else. In one three-month period in prison, he lost eight pounds. Maybe he has Crohn's disease, one friend speculated. It was hard to tell from his medical records. Ailments surged up and then disappeared without a trace. One note he wrote reads:

MEDICAL NEED (Necesidad Medica/Bezwen Medikal):

I can sleep all time

Make Dream like to kill somebody

i need more sleeping pill fore sleep never go sleep for ever

Mental hleath

As I looked through Chuol's file I kept checking my watch. The trial was due to begin at 2 p.m. Eastern Time — 9 p.m. on the Kenyan coast. I joined the virtual courtroom early, only to hear Chuol's lawyer chatting with his DHS counterpart. When I first started doing deportation cases, the degree of collaboration between what I thought were dueling opponents shocked me. The final decisions always felt like a conversation—a way of getting the two lawyers and the judge to agree together on a reasonable account of what should happen. Nothing about this felt reasonable. How could they discuss deporting someone who had only known America— and encountered the core of America's problems, the racism and the homelessness and the willful blindness—to a country that didn't even exist when Chuol last set foot in Africa, sixteen years ago? The lawyers were talking like old friends.

> DHS: If he gets DCAT, we might just send him to Libya.
>
> Chuol's lawyer: Who is handling the removal proceedings from Djibouti? [Eight migrants were being held there, pending legal appeal, on their way to South Sudan, though most of them—Vietnamese and Laotians among their number—had no link to the country.]

When the lawyers realized I was online, their friendly chatter ceased.

The courtroom was one square of the virtual grid. Another was occupied by Chuol's translator. Chuol himself was absent. He had been transferred to Texas, and the prison guards didn't seem able to get him to a conference room to attend his own hearing. Regardless, the case continued. The DHS lawyer had been tardy in filing some paperwork, and the judge berated him. "When there are no consequences for actions, then people will do whatever they want," she told the courtroom.

After I was called to the virtual stand and swore my oath, I had to prove my eligibility to be an expert witness. After twenty years of working as a conflict researcher in the Sudans, I've always been recognized. The DHS lawyer seemed resigned to letting me testify, and only wanted to insist that—as must be obvious—I am not an expert in mental health. He proffered this point as a gotcha, as if it invalidated what I was about to say.

Chuol's lawyer opened proceedings. Most immigration lawyers are harried and harassed, with too many cases and not enough time. If they have country of origin expertise, it is in Central America, not the Horn of Africa. Chuol's lawyer was no exception, and while I have no legal training, I thought his questions were poor. The Padang Dinka, the group from which Chuol hails, were being forcibly recruited into government militias.

Instead of asking me about this, and so establishing the particularity of Chuol's situation, the lawyer simply noted that militia recruitment *in general* was ongoing in South Sudan—a point the DHS would later seize upon in cross-examination to establish that the risk to Chuol was no greater than that posed to the general population. "He might be recruited," the DHS lawyer claimed, "but only because everyone will be recruited." In her ruling, the judge would primly note that "sovereign nations have the right to enforce laws of conscription and penalties for evasion."

After a cursory examination by Chuol's lawyer, my cross-examination was held up for a moment: Chuol had finally arrived in the virtual courtroom. He wore an oversized orange jumpsuit, and nodded as his translator briefly explained the case to him. A prison guard slumbered on a chair nearby.

If Chuol dies like other Sudanese or South Sudanese, the DHS lawyer continued, it's not personal.

During cross-examination, the DHS lawyer acknowledged that while Dr. Craze had shown there are almost no mental health facilities in South Sudan, and those that did exist in Sudan had been destroyed by the civil war, and while yes, he conceded, there was only one psychiatric ward in Juba, South Sudan's capital, with only twelve beds (three were recently broken and there was no money to replace them), and while yes, he admitted, in Juba, if you were lucky and mentally ill, you went to the central prison, and got chained, naked, to the floor on which you defecated, in a dark room devoted to "the lunatics," he insisted that we should not be in the business of looking down at African standards of care. That the mentally ill were beaten with rubber hoses spiked with plastic fragments went unmentioned during his remarks. The judge later noted in her final judgment that "torture does not include . . . gross overcrowding and inadequate access to food, potable water, sanitation, heating, ventilation, lighting, or medical care."

The cross-examination became a grandstanding performance by the DHS lawyer. It might be the case, he continued, that there is a civil war in Sudan, and a counterinsurgency in South Sudan, and both countries might be in the grip of humanitarian crises, but if Chuol dies like other Sudanese or South Sudanese, then he is simply dying, and he is not dying because he is Chuol, because of some special reason, some special thing, that makes him Chuol. It's not personal. He is just dead. And as he will die, just like other Sudanese, he is not eligible for DCAT.

Chuol was unmoving, entirely mute.

After the cross-examination concluded, there was no redirect from Chuol's lawyer. I was told that I could leave, but I stayed on to hear the closing arguments.

Chuol's lawyer took less than five minutes to argue for DCAT. His phrasing was generic. There was a civil war in Sudan. Conditions were bad. Chuol shouldn't be deported.

The DHS lawyer, in closing, made what seemed like an entirely spurious argument. Yes, Dr. Craze has shown that it is likely that security officers will burn Chuol with cigarettes. Yes, he will be beaten with sticks and rubber hoses. That is unfortunate. But if Chuol is indeed detained by national security at the airport after being deported, he will likely not be kept in detention for long, because he is a nobody, a nothing, not a rebel, and so not a threat to the government. (It was no longer clear, at this point, if the lawyer was talking about Sudan or South Sudan, not that anyone seemed to mind.) Because Chuol will likely be quickly released from detention, he will not have been burned with sufficient cigarettes for it to constitute torture.

The whole farce took two hours. The judge declared that she would make a decision within thirty-one days. She told Chuol, "I will never see you again, but I will pass my judgement to your lawyer." Chuol's translator didn't translate the message. The screen went black.

A month later, on July 8, the judge ruled that Chuol was inadmissible for DCAT. He would be, as the ruling put it, "REMOVED to South Sudan or Sudan." **BR**

TWO RAIDS ON CANAL STREET

Liv Veazey

THROUGH VIDEOS CIRCULATING among Senegalese friends in WhatsApp chats, I watched the October 21 ICE raid unfold on New York City's Canal Street. It was a spectacle: herds of ICE agents in tactical vests and neck gaiters shrink-wrapped to their faces fanned out around a hulking armored vehicle, the purpose of which was unclear. I recognized a few masked agents from last summer, when we had stood in arms' reach of one another in immigration court: over time, I'd come to know the contours of certain noses and lips beneath certain sets of eyes, a particular gait paired with a particular ballcap logo. One of them, I realized, was the same man who had shoved a woman to the ground in immigration court a few weeks prior, an act for which he'd been briefly suspended. Now, apparently, he was back on the streets.

For the past five months we had seen the way federal agents laid claim to other cities. The National Guard descended on Los Angeles and ICE rappelled from a Black Hawk into a Chicago apartment complex. As we watched, we tried to guess when the same force would land on the streets of New York.

At this point, most New Yorkers had seen the images of federal agents crowding the hallways of immigration courtrooms, the roundups in Home Depot parking lots, the four-person ICE squads waiting outside of apartment buildings in Queens and South Brooklyn. But if you didn't need to attend ICE check-ins or live in targeted neighborhoods, you may not have seen an agent in the city with your own eyes. Operation Canal Street brought ICE's presence out into the open, in the middle of downtown Manhattan, for everyone to see.

The intersection of Canal and Broadway is a strategic location for ICE to stage a raid. It's a straight, five-minute walk from 26 Federal Plaza, the facility where ICE often holds people they've just arrested in New York City. Drive five minutes west and you'll enter the Holland Tunnel, on the other side of which is Delaney Hall in New Jersey, a private detention center that, after reopening under a $1 billion, fifteen-year ICE contract in 2025, provides an extra one thousand beds for ICE detainees, quadrupling the state's immigration detention capacity.

Canal Street is also the location of a decades-old gray market for counterfeit goods whose sidewalks are lined with Chinese, West African, and Bangladeshi vendors selling hats, watches, wallets, and shades for highly negotiable prices. Their presence attracts hordes of international tourists, most of them wealthy and European—as well as, I've been told by vendors, NYPD officers looking for nice gifts for their mothers-in-law.

It seems that ICE's primary objective was less to get bodies inside of prison cells and more to be seen and filmed.

On the day of the raid, some vendors were tipped off and stayed home. As the agents jog-walked around the armored vehicle, black and red pepperball launchers clasped to their chests, the remaining sellers scrambled to pack up their merchandise before scattering. Bystanders turned their heads and watched the agents make their way up onto the sidewalk, where they circled around targets to demand their papers. One Black man with a Brooklyn accent yells, "I'm not doin' nothin'! I'm from Brooklyn!" as two Homeland Security agents press him against a wall, one running his hands down the man's arms and legs. As they began making arrests, ICE officers spawned dozens of spontaneous protesters. In response, one agent brought out a yellow taser, holding it in front of his face and pointing it at anyone in his way before shoving them aside.

All told, the agents detained only nine people on the grounds of their suspected immigration status. Given the relatively small number of captures, it seems that ICE's primary objective was less to get bodies inside of prison cells and more to be seen and filmed—and for those videos to sow confidence or fear, depending on the watcher.

It's possible the raid was triggered by videos from right-wing YouTubers, one of whom was Nick Shirley, now famous for terrorizing Somali daycare center workers in Minneapolis with clips watched and amplified by top Trump administration figures. About a month before ICE appeared on Canal Street, Shirley posted a video walking down its busy sidewalks. In the video, one vendor offers Shirley AirPods. When

Shirley asks how he got them, the vendor explains street markets: "Anywhere in the world there is a market [the video's subtitles read "black market," but that's not what the man says] where people can get anything they want for a cheap price."

Shirley calls the vendors "scam artists." In reality, no one thinks they're buying real products: vendors exist because of market demand, an insatiable appetite for lookalike Louis Vuitton bags that compels the underemployed—many of whom are shut out of formal and salaried work—onto the street. The promise of a swarm of shoppers around a vendor's tarp when he pulls out a fresh set of faux Rolexes and YSL shades draws him to this work, with its risks of exposure and arrest.

One of the men who was detained during the raid told me that he heard the federal agents discussing Shirley's YouTube video. Shirley himself was present that day, too, there to film a follow-up. Part of ICE's expanded budget includes $100 million earmarked for promotional contracts with influencers: a small army of Nick Shirleys, cameras in hand, ready to clear the ideological ground for the next raid.

The following day, DHS posted grainy mugshots of the nine people it arrested on its X page, naming all except one a "criminal illegal alien." A friend of one of the detained men told me he had looked into getting his image taken down, but abandoned the effort after a lawyer said it would cost thousands of dollars.

THE FIRST RAID DEMONSTRATED ICE's imperious will to be seen. At the second raid a month later, a small army of observers gathered in response. In the days before the operation, tips circulated among the group chats of ICE watchers, and warnings were translated to French, Wolof, and Mandarin. Vendors began their own countersurveillance, sending videos and photographs of suspicious clients to vet them after rumors circulated that plainclothes ICE agents were buying counterfeit merchandise to be used as evidence for future arrests.

When a suspicious figure approached, vendors whispered to each other, in a kind of telephone game that filtered down the sidewalks of Little Italy, *"Mafia, mafia, mafia."* It was a term that new West African asylees had learned to use after their encounters with Mexican police extorting them on their journeys towards the southern U.S. border. For them, *mafia* had come to mean any shadowy force posing a threat to the collective: in New York, such forces included police officers, journalists, companies like Uber or DoorDash, United States Citizenship and Immigration Services, scam lawyers, and increasingly, the American government writ large.

On the day of the second raid, I was on the other side of the country, but through videos and photos I constructed a shaky iPhone collage of the entire event. Dozens of federal agents had staged their vans in a parking garage off Canal Street. Protestors surrounded the vehicles, blocking them in. A wall of agents stood looking out from the garage's open entrance, their ranks extending back into the shadows, visible by the glints of light on tinted sunglasses. Those at the front waited with wide stances, arms hanging at their sides, swaying and fidgeting.

At first, they were remarkably still, as if waiting for a cue, while the growing crowd of protesters, chanting, willed them out of the city. Then the agents advanced, pushing against a crowd that refused to budge. When the NYPD arrived, responding to a call that the street was being obstructed, they began making arrests. Police officers erected metal barricades to cordon off protestors, while protesters dragged potted trees out in front of ICE vans to block them from pulling out.

At the end of the day, although more than a dozen people were taken into NYPD custody, nobody had been detained by immigration enforcement. Flashing police vans filled with protestors carved a slow path of retreat through the crowd, clearing the way for ICE vans filled only with ICE agents. By any measure, the second raid was unsuccessful, stymied by a mass mobilization of watchers whose numbers have grown alongside DHS's ballooning payroll.

A MONTH LATER, from a windowless room in One World Trade Center, Kristi Noem, Secretary of Homeland Security, and Frank Russo, New York's Director of Field Operations for Customs and Border Protection, held a press conference to tout the success of Operation Salvo, a series of arrests targeting fifty-four people allegedly affiliated with the Trinitarios gang. For the occasion, ICE had printed posters with yet more grainy mugshots, this time of young Dominican men, with text above each photo reading ARRESTED, designed to look like a rubber stamp. "The best thing about this operation," Russo told reporters, "is that it was done the way law enforcement loves to do it: quietly, discreetly, behind the scenes. Often under the cover of darkness."

Part of ICE's expanded budget includes $100 million earmarked for promotional contracts with influencers.

Those tactics are a far cry from the first raid on Canal Street, with its midday military procession down a commercial thoroughfare, or similar operations across the country. In ever-proliferating videos of agents with their knees on the necks of teenagers, or taking their batons to car windows and dragging out drivers across broken glass, the visual evidence captured by ICE watchers is at odds with the agency's claim to quiet, discreet, and thus more orderly and precise enforcement.

Officers often claim that those filming them are disrupting their work, even when distance is maintained. Agents insist that the watchers step back. Observation itself, they suggest, is an obstruction. ICE wants it both ways: to be seen swooping in to return law and order to American streets, but to do so anonymously, faces hidden. The watchers see past the spectacle of the military parade, focusing our attention on the moments the agency would rather conceal: a girl managing to get safely inside her house, closing the door behind her moments before men lumbering in pursuit can reach her out on the icy sidewalk; four agents carrying the limp body of an unconscious protester, limbs bent unnaturally, head lolling forward.

Noem and Russo were speaking just a few blocks south of the parking garage where ICE had spent an afternoon surrounded by immigrants yet unable to make a single arrest. Almost all the questions posed to Noem were about one person; her name was being chanted by a crowd of protesters on the sidewalk below. She was someone who, despite the immense capaciousness of the term, did not fall into the category of immigrant, and whose final act was watching: Renee Nicole Good. **BR**

RENEE GOOD'S MURDER AND OTHER ACTS OF TERROR

Robin D. G. Kelley with Deborah Chasman

*O***N JANUARY 7** *U.S. Immigration and Customs Enforcement (ICE) agent Jonathan Ross shot and killed Renee Good, a thirty-seven-year-old woman who had been observing ICE raids from her car in her Minneapolis neighborhood. In videos of the incident, we can see Ross firing through Good's windshield and open window as she begins to drive away. The horrific footage of the killing felt like a stark symbol of today's authoritarian moment—but at the same time, I knew that anyone involved in the struggle against police violence would find it tragically familiar.*

To put Good's killing in context, I spoke with historian and Boston Review *contributing editor Robin D. G. Kelley, whose forthcoming book,* Making a Killing: Capitalism, Cops, and the War on Black Life, *covers the history of county, state, and municipal police violence—as well as the activism against it. In an email exchange on January 15, we discussed the pitfalls of the "perfect-victim narrative," policing's terror tactics, why agents don't need more training, and where we go from here.*

Just a week after this interview was first published, ICE murdered nurse Alex Pretti in Minneapolis—further escalating protests, as well as demands from Democrats that the agency be reformed. Kelley's words make clear that the "guardrails" the party is pursuing will do nothing for public safety.

—Deborah Chasman, coeditor-in-chief

DEBORAH CHASMAN: Good's killing shocked Americans. But much about it reflects violence that's very familiar to you. Can you put the murder in the context of your research?

ROBIN D. G. KELLEY: Despite having spent more than thirty years studying and writing about police violence, I am still shocked by every death—even when the outcome is predictable. But the killing of Good shocked even the most seasoned organizers. She was a white woman and a mother—two things you're not supposed to be when armed agents of the state put you in a body bag. (That she was queer and a poet, not so much.)

Of course, the very idea that certain people, by virtue of their characteristics, don't deserve to be brutalized, caged, or killed by police is the problem. Mariame Kaba warns against "perfect-victim narratives," which reinforce what Ruth Wilson Gilmore calls "the problem of innocence." Centering someone's innocence clouds the case for abolition, which seeks to create a world where no one is caged or gunned down even if they broke the law. No matter who she was, what she looked like, her marital or citizenship status, or what she might have done in the past or even in the moment, Good had the absolute right not to be shot for driving away.

What doesn't surprise me is why and how Jonathan Ross shot her and the federal government's efforts to cover up what happened. Researching *Making a Killing*, I found too many incidents to count where police fatally shot people for attempting to drive away. These were not high-speed chases, by the way—sometimes it was just a car lurching forward or an engine revving up that prompted a shooting. They all have one thing in common: police justify the shootings as *acts of self-defense*. The alleged "suspect," the story goes, intended to ram the officer, who opened fire because he feared for his life. After these shootings, cops rarely argue they were simply trying to stop a fleeing suspect, because it opens them up to two objections: that firing at a driver puts others in harm's way, and that they could have taken down the license plate and pursued the person later. Fearing for one's life is always used to absolve cops from having to explain why they didn't act differently.

This is why, in videos of the moments before the shooting, we can hear Good's wife Rebecca saying, "We don't change our plates every morning, just so you know. It will be the same plate when you come talk to us later." And this is also why, for many years and in different cities, movements fighting police misconduct demanded that officers be banned from using lethal force against fleeing suspects who do not pose an imminent threat, whether on foot or in a car.

I'm also not shocked by the utter refusal of the federal government to investigate or consider bringing charges against Ross. I've lived through and documented so many cases of officers whose egregious acts of violence led to no indictments and no investigations, so many cases of police and even prosecutors destroying incriminating evidence. The question is, why are so many people surprised and indignant about the feds' unqualified defense of Ross? Maybe because we've fallen into the trap of distinguishing ICE and CBP (bad) from local police (good). Maybe it's a residual effect of the January 6 insurrection, in which some police officers had been victims of right-wing mobs (which themselves included a disproportionate number of cops and soldiers). In any case, the narrative has taken hold that ICE agents are rogue cops or cops on steroids, trained to terrorize or simply untrained. Strangest of all in this story is the liberal pipe dream that local police will stand up against ICE and CBP, when police have collaborated with ICE and been deployed to protect agents from protesters, even in so-called sanctuary cities.

I'm not sure if it's amnesia or just wishful thinking, but it seems like the well-documented terror tactics of municipal, county, and state police have just disappeared from people's memory. Chicago and Los Angeles, where resistance to ICE has been extraordinary and well-organized, have histories of police violence that rival anything ICE agents are doing. Indeed, it is precisely the long experience of organizing against this violence that prepared activists in these cities to resist ICE.

Chicago, which takes up a very long chapter in my book, is known for police torture, the maintenance of secret "black sites," assassinations and executions, and prosecutors who have consistently protected police even to the point of hiding evidence. This is the city where the second Black police superintendent, LeRoy Martin, bragged in 1987, "When you talk about gangs, I've got the toughest gang in town: the Chicago Police Department." And it is the same city that has been a model of resistance to police repression for more than half a century, culminating in the collective struggles for justice for Rekia Boyd, Laquan McDonald, and victims of torture that brought down the ruling regime of Rahm Emanuel.

This is not to diminish ICE and CBP's violent tactics. These outright abductions are terrifying, though again, not without precedent. Police have abducted Black men standing on a street corner or a stoop and tossed them into unmarked vans just for looking suspicious, and there are numerous cases of young Black women abducted off the streets and sexually assaulted by police. But there is a fundamental difference between these abductions and ICE's: the former were intended to be secret, the latter publicized. ICE and CBP agents are either filming these acts of terror themselves (Ross had one hand on his gun and the other holding his cell phone to film!), or they are arriving with a film crew. The point is to create fear, to terrorize people into submission, to create a state of emergency.

Finally, let's try not to make these attacks about Trump or even Stephen Miller. Both ICE and CBP have histories of violence dating back to well before 2016. My colleague Kelly Lytle Hernández has written on the history of the Border Patrol, which has been terrorizing people since 1924.

DC: Republicans and right-wing pundits have been relentless in blaming Good for her murder, or calling her a domestic terrorist and warning that any activism will put you in harm's way. Clearly there's a legal element to blaming Good—it's meant to exonerate the agent. But how do those narratives function politically?

RK: Anyone organizing against state power will be a target, whether their protest abides by the law or involves civil disobedience. Either way, nothing justifies the harm, which is what these narratives attempt to do. Just last night, after ICE shot another person in Minnesota and protesters were in the streets battling federal agents, there was a lot of talk—including from Governor Tim Walz and Minneapolis Mayor Jacob Frey—about the need for peaceful protest: code for candlelight vigils and silent prayer. Militant civil disobedience, aggressively confronting a phalanx of masked agents in riot gear, or blocking traffic is nonviolent, but these tactics are not considered by the political class to count as "peaceful protest." And by now, it should be clear that peaceful protest, whatever form it takes, will not get ICE or CBP out of your city; it will not stop the terror or the abductions.

And yet, when we return to Good's death, we must remember that she actually wasn't protesting. She was a legal observer doing her job, and when told to leave she was complying. Unsurprisingly, J. D. Vance and all the right-wingers who blame Good for her death are simply lying. Calling her a domestic terrorist—it's the oldest trick in the book. The subtext to which we ought to pay attention is how her gender and sexuality constituted the real threat to Ross, his fellow agents, Vance, Stephen Miller, and MAGA. One must imagine what it meant to Ross for a smiling queer woman to tell him, "I'm not mad at you." After shooting her three times, Ross or an agent near him mutters, "Fucking bitch!" That says it all.

Nearly every victim of an ICE or CBP shooting is blamed by being labeled either a fugitive or domestic terrorist. When ICE agents fatally shot Silverio Villegas-González, a thirty-eight-year-old immigrant from Mexico, as he tried to drive away from what amounted to an ambush in Chicago, DHS released a brazenly false statement claiming that he "refused to follow law enforcement officers' commands" and used his car as a weapon, hitting and dragging one of the officers. And so the same old story goes: "Fearing for his own life and broader public safety, the officer fired his weapon." We know now that no officer was hit or dragged, and the one officer that was allegedly hurt suffered minor cuts from breaking Villegas-González's window.

Likewise, when CBP agents shot Marimar Martinez, a thirty-year-old schoolteacher and U.S. citizen—also in Chicago—they labeled her a domestic terrorist and charged her with ramming a federal law enforcement officer. We know now that the agent, Charles Exum, rammed *her* vehicle, jumped out with his gun drawn, and said "Do something bitch" before shooting her five times. The DHS lies were so egregious (and Exum didn't help their case by bragging about it in text messages) that the prosecution had no choice but to drop all the charges.

DC: In the wake of Good's murder, many have called for better training for ICE officers—a response that activist Kelly Hayes and others have forcefully rejected. I know you agree with Hayes. Can you explain why?

RK: Ross wasn't one of those cats recruited with a $50,000 bonus and handed a gun. Besides being a veteran of the Iraq war, he had spent a decade as a member of the special response team of ICE's enforcement and removal operation. He got more training than most of the other masked goons running the streets of the Twin Cities. The argument for more and better training was thoroughly discredited after George Floyd's murder in 2020. As it turned out, Derek Chauvin had lots of training: he had taken the crisis intervention training, use-of-force training, de-escalation vs. restraint training, and even training in implicit bias, which became mandatory for Minneapolis police officers beginning in 2018. The result? Chauvin racked up seventeen misconduct complaints over nineteen years on the force. And after 2018, cases of police brutality and excessive force complaints increased across the city.

But if training hasn't worked, why does it continue? Why is it always trotted out, alongside new technologies, as *the* solution? Because training and technologies (body cams, Tasers, so-called less-than-lethal weapons, predictive policing software) are a boondoggle for corporate interests. Training costs money, which increases police budgets, which are paid for through taxes and bonds—a hidden source of revenue for financial institutions that administer the bonds. The money for training flows to private companies, usually run by former police chiefs and so-called criminal justice experts—not community organizations that have been fighting for accountability. Sometimes the investment in new technologies and training comes from corporate-funded private police foundations, whose donations enable departments to purchase equipment, such as surveillance technology, guns, ballistic helmets, cameras, and drones, and assist officers with bonuses or legal fees, with no oversight or public input. But corporations like Amazon and Google get a great return on their investment since law enforcement agencies adopt technologies of surveillance, data mining and management, etc., coming from these companies.

To understand what "training" produces, let's focus on one company: 21st Century Policing Solutions, LLC (21CP), which grew directly out of an Obama-era task force formed in late 2014 after the killing of Michael Brown. 21CP is made up of law enforcement officials, lawyers, and academics, and it's paid by municipalities and university public safety forces to train police in a host of areas: gaining community trust, racial equity, changing use-of-force policies, communication, transparency, strategic management, and community policing. Usually, this work entails producing reports that ultimately just repeat boilerplate recommendations. Oklahoma City paid 21CP $193,000 for a report many Black residents found to be useless—nothing changed. Aurora, Colorado, paid 21CP $340,000 to "investigate" the police missteps that resulted in the death of Elijah McClain, a young Black man who had been injected with ketamine under police custody and died. 21CP produced a 161-page report that primarily described the operations of the Aurora Police Department, compared it with other departments in similar-sized cities, repeated what we all know about the death of McClain, and offered obvious and fairly innocuous recommendations: prohibiting chokeholds, retaliatory violence, using force on people who are handcuffed—in other words, prohibiting behavior that is already prohibited. And worse, these reports often suggest recruiting and training *more* officers. I want to suggest that when we talk about training and technology, we need to follow the money. And in the case of CBP and ICE, the last thing we should be doing is proposing reforms that give them more money.

As the coercive arm of the state, the police—including CBP and ICE—are the primary instruments of state violence within the borders of the United States. They function as an occupying force in America's impoverished ghettos, barrios, reservations, on the Southwest border, and in any territory with high concentrations of subjugated communities. For people who reside in these communities, keeping us safe is not the objective. Instead, the modern police force—whether local, state, or federal—wages domestic war. Whether we call it a war on crime, a war on militants, or a war on drugs, law enforcement at every level has turned many Black working-class neighborhoods in particular into killing fields and open-air prisons, stripping vulnerable residents of equal protection, habeas corpus, freedom of movement, and even protection from torture. The attack on nonwhite immigrants is just another front in a war the police have waged since their inception.

And despite the handwringing and outrage over the Trump administration's flagrant violation of the Posse Comitatus Act of 1878 limiting the use of the military in domestic matters, the police have long functioned as an army against dissident social movements. The police are the first line of defense against strikes and left-wing protests, while often serving as a cordon to protect Klansman, Nazis, and the alt-right.

DC: What are the chances that Ross will be held accountable? How does this end?

RK: Simply put, Ross will not be held accountable, nor will anyone else responsible for the death or injury of victims of ICE or CBP attacks. As I document in my book, we can't get accountability from the "regular" police, whatever that means: after decades, we haven't been able to achieve something as basic as an honest civilian review board with subpoena powers and the ability to hire and fire officers! Since Trump's second term, things have gotten even worse. Guided by the Heritage Foundation's Project 2025, the Trump administration rescinded Biden-era police and criminal justice reforms; shuttered the National Law Enforcement Accountability Database

(NLEAD) created in 2023 to allow prospective employers to access the records of federal law enforcement officers in order to check their backgrounds for misconduct; halted all open federal investigations into law enforcement, notably in Jackson, Mississippi, and New York City; ended federal consent decrees mandating reforms of Louisville and Minneapolis police departments; made the extraordinary offer of free private-sector legal services for officers accused of misconduct.

It is not enough to abolish ICE. We need to abolish the police and cages and build other institutions and relationships that can bring us genuine safety. Abolition is less an act of demolition than a construction project. It is creative creation, the boundless, boundary-less struggle to make our collective lives better, what Gilmore calls "life in rehearsal."

Ironically, the federal government's escalation of violence and its spillover into other communities have actually forced people to find their own strategies to keep each other safe, through communication, patrols, whistles, trainings in nonviolent resistance, and old-fashioned organizing. It's not just about keeping ICE out, but making sure that the medical and child care needs of neighbors are being met, that people who can't leave their homes out of fear are fed, and that some homes can become designated safe houses.

I'm reminded of a 2009 statement issued by the abolitionist organization Critical Resistance. Instead of police, the statement asks,

> What if we got together with members of our communities and created systems of support for each other? . . . Relying on and deploying policing denies our ability to do this, to create real safety in our communities.

We're seeing this in action now in the mobilizations against ICE. The question is whether it can be sustained and turned into something that can replace our dependence on armed agents of the state to solve human problems. **BR**

A U.S. Navy strike group enters the Caribbean Sea. Image: Getty Images

THE PATH TO THE TRUMP DOCTRINE

Aslı Ü. Bâli & Aziz Rana

I N LATE 2024, the world watched with a mix of hope and disbelief as opposition forces in Syria finally toppled Bashar al-Assad, ending more than fifty years of rule by the Assad family. Images of rebel fighters throwing open the gates of the notorious Sednaya prison, where thousands had been detained, tortured, and killed under the old government, symbolized a break from a past defined by repression and mass killing. Opposition leader Ahmed al-Sharaa declared the beginning of "a new chapter in the history of the region," and in the months that followed, it seemed like that old hope might finally be realized. Several countries—including the United States—eased sanctions to support Syria's fragile democratic transition. And by November 2025 al-Sharaa was standing in the Oval Office, where even President Donald Trump expressed something like cautious optimism. "We want to see Syria become a country that's very successful," he said. "We have all had rough pasts."

In theory, the fall of Assad created a moment for reconstruction and renewed sovereignty. In reality, Syria's transition would fall swiftly under American supervision. The Trump administration spent the second half of 2025 forging new arrangements for managing Syria in partnership with Israel, drawing up a security pact in which Syrian forces would withdraw from the border region and allow for the opening of an air corridor for Israel to strike Iran. Negotiations remain ongoing to finalize the details, but the core elements underscore the double edge of the opportunity presented by Assad's toppling: while the new Syrian leadership seeks to end regional isolation, the proposed agreements risk turning Damascus into a client state.

If 2025 opened with the hope—albeit quickly dashed—that the United States might encourage local sovereignty, the first days of

2026 witnessed that hope's stark opposite: the sudden, forcible removal of a sitting head of state. After an abduction operation that apparently involved the killing of over a hundred people on Venezuelan soil, U.S. officials declared Venezuelan president Nicolás Maduro was in American custody, a fact quickly confirmed by a photo of a blindfolded Maduro in a U.S. Navy ship. A gloating Trump proclaimed the United States would now "run Venezuela" and take control of the country's oil.

It was a stunning action, but not necessarily a surprising one. A month earlier, the Trump administration had hinted at its future plans in its National Security Strategy, a thirty-three-page manifesto-like statement of its foreign policy priorities. The document frankly describes the world in terms of "global and regional balances of power," highlighting the need for the United States to redefine its economic relationship with China while framing the challenge in Europe as one of managing the continent's relations with Russia. It largely abandons the post–Cold War language of multilateralism and liberal internationalism, replacing that language with a blunt, transactional vision of national interest and hemispheric dominance. And it presents the Western Hemisphere as a region to be dominated under the "Trump Corollary" to the Monroe Doctrine—or as he calls it, the Donroe Doctrine.

Unlike earlier American framings, Trump's embrace of conditional sovereignty suggests an approach where the United States stands first in a multipolar world of authoritarian hegemons and operates independent of longstanding American self-understanding with respect to democracy or the rule of law. This approach sees the globe as divided among "civilizationally" distinct ethno-national communities. And the explicitness of its embrace of quid pro quo arrangements and hard power alone renders quaint the long-familiar talk of international law. U.S. action now depends on raw threat rather than the classic combination of hard and soft power, where force proceeded alongside legitimating narratives and consensus-building. Under the Trump doctrine, "America First" suggests two claims: a domestic ethno-racial identity that asserts a fortress wall against immigrants, and continued global dominance where the strongest stick presides over a lawless order.

Today, Trump and those around him openly talk about annexing Greenland, Canada, and the Panama Canal, gloat over extrajudicial killings in the Caribbean and the Pacific, threaten to seize rare-earth minerals in the Democratic Republic of the Congo and oil in Venezuela, abduct foreign heads of state, and suggest similar actions—along with potential regime change—across the Americas and the world, from Iran to Cuba, Nicaragua, Colombia, and even Mexico. All the while, they muse over the benefits of Palestinian ethnic cleansing, impose sanctions on jurists— foreign and international—that seek accountability for war crimes or gross human rights abuses, use tariff threats to extract global resources, and treat white South Africans as the world's only worthy refugees. What brought us to this point?

DEPENDING ON YOUR VANTAGE POINT, the Trump doctrine appears either strikingly new or eerily familiar. Beltway commentators rushed to label the National Security Strategy a "radical departure" from the U.S.-led post-World War II era. Others saw its mirror in the nine- teenth-century gunboat diplomacy of U.S. naval coercion from Japan to the Caribbean. And critics to the left were quick to underscore its links to the long trail of U.S. imperialism, from Cold War rivalries in the Global South to the more recent terms of the war on terror. In many ways, the best reading is one that underscores both continuity and rupture.

Trump sees the United States standing first in a world divided among "civilizationally" distinct ethno-national communities.

If there was a break from the past, it began long before January 2025. For one thing, the post-1945 liberal international order has always been marked by legal restraint and self-interested defection, the cre- ation of human rights bodies and the embrace of coups, assassinations and armed overthrows. In the last twenty-five years, those defections have swallowed the rule. In Afghanistan and Iraq, the United States ren- dered sovereignty negotiable and transformed the universal premises of the postwar order into something far narrower: a reconfigured world subject to American prerogatives, conditions, and tutelage. Trump has now pushed this logic past its breaking point, by directly attacking even the institutions that would sustain international law for other states. Today, the country is not simply defecting from the rules—expanding the zone of exception for itself—but acting to make those rules fundamentally inoperable.

The path to Trump 2.0 is long and winding, but to understand its most proximate influences we need only look back a couple of presidents—especially to their actions in the Middle East. Barack Obama may have been celebrated for his commitment to liberal internationalism, and in many ways, he did embody its last gasp. Even so, his administration designed a system of targeted killing through drone strikes in the Muslim world that purported to legalize extrajudicial executions at the sole discretion of the U.S. president. Trump's killings at sea take such Obama-era lawlessness as their clear precedent.

After Trump's first term, the Biden presidency was billed a return to normalcy with respect to international law and global responsibility. Yet instead of resurrecting the old order, Biden cemented its end, exemplified by his refusal to apply either U.S. or international law to Gaza—even in the face of a drumbeat of official resignations.

In 2021, he came into office declaring that "America is back" and "ready to lead the world," asserting a "values-based" approach to foreign policy that evoked the days of postwar internationalism. As it turned out, the change was more one of tone than substance. In press conferences and statements, Biden liked to invoke a nostalgic image of Cold War American multilateralism (one that conveniently omitted all those interventions and coups). Yet the centerpiece of "winning hearts and minds" during the Cold War had been massive material investments to woo potential allies, embodied through projects such as the Marshall Plan. And while Biden did reestablish some funding for organizations like the World Health Organization (WHO), his administration was skeptical of the WHO's new investment round and related funding reforms, both backed by a cross-section of Europe and the Global South.

Neither did Biden slow the decades-long decline of U.S. foreign aid as a percentage of GDP, let alone suggest any real dedication to spreading American largesse—an attitude highlighted by the terms of his much-touted exit from Afghanistan. The United States may have pumped billions of dollars into the country, but often through defense contracting that enriched U.S. companies without materially improving the lives of Afghans or building legitimacy for U.S.-backed institutions. When Biden ordered troops to leave the country, he left behind a record of broken promises and local allies bereft of protection, all of which reduced grand U.S. rhetoric to cheap talk.

At the same time, the Biden administration embraced its own aggressive posturing and rule-breaking. It essentially kept in place the hardline Trump policies toward Cuba, undermining trade and travel and further isolating the country after the Obama-era détente. And despite claims to the contrary, it never recommitted to the signature foreign policy accomplishment of those Obama years, the 2015 Iran nuclear deal, from which Trump had unilaterally withdrawn. Instead, Biden continued to blanket Tehran with harsh sanctions.

BUT BIDEN'S MOST VISIBLE CONTINUATION of the Trump 1.0 approach came in the so-called "pivot to Asia." When Biden entered office, he sought to complete a project that had eluded his two predecessors: recentering American grand strategy around long-term technological, military, and economic competition with China while extricating the United States from its oversight of wars and resource dependencies in the Middle East. China's rise, the logic went, was the structural challenge of this century. The United States continued to have significant strategic interests in the Middle East: preserving Israel's military hegemony, containing Iran, and maintaining privileged access to the Gulf's energy resources. But direct presence in the region had real diminishing returns, given the opportunity costs. The Biden administration's foreign-policy triage—withdraw from Afghanistan, downgrade the region, and redirect attention to the Indo-Pacific—was meant to consolidate American power for a new era of system-level rivalry.

From the start, Biden consciously followed both Obama and Trump's lead in his adversarial approach to China. His administration re-energized the Quad with Japan, Australia, and India; launched the security partnership AUKUS to embed Britain and Australia in the Pacific security architecture; and passed industrial-policy packages—most notably the CHIPS and Inflation Reduction Acts—designed to promote U.S.

innovation beyond Beijing while increasingly boxing China out of access to critical technologies. The goal was to contain China without overt confrontation (though Biden's commitment to Taiwan and military-first approach to the South China Sea did little to turn down the heat).

All of this would soon give way to global overstretch. The first snag was Russia's invasion of Ukraine in 2022, which led Washington to re-militarize NATO and sustain a massive flow of weapons and intelligence to Europe. Still, by mid-2023, the White House believed it had stabilized the transatlantic front and could finally execute the eastward shift. Its marquee initiative—the India-Middle East-Europe Economic Corridor (IMEC), unveiled at the New Delhi G20 summit—was conceived as the infrastructural complement to the pivot: a U.S.-led alternative to China's Belt and Road Initiative.

Biden's practices in the Middle East already demonstrated the extent to which Pax Americana was disintegrating.

IMEC, which aimed to connect South Asia, the Gulf, and Europe through Israel's ports, formed the economic wing of the realignment project Biden inherited from Trump: if successful, it would fulfill the Abraham Accords' vision of normalizing relations between Israel and Arab nations by courting Saudi Arabia. But it was precisely the Accords' dream of a new, Israel-centered order for the Middle East that foreshadowed the unraveling of Biden's strategy. October 7 and the invasion of Gaza forced the administration into an all-consuming crisis that upended every premise of the pivot. While Biden administration officials regularly assured global audiences that they were working "tirelessly" to achieve a ceasefire, the United States, once the self-styled indispensable mediator, was bankrolling and facilitating the Israeli military campaign behind the scenes. Instead of downsizing its Middle East footprint, Washington's "ironclad" commitment to Israel became the defining feature of its foreign policy and global posture.

The war's timing was catastrophic for Biden's grand design. On October 6—the day before the Hamas attack—U.S. officials were meeting Saudi diplomats to finalize what they believed could be a historic bargain: normalization between Israel and Riyadh. The entire enterprise rested on the Abraham Accords' illusion that the Palestinian question could be managed and sidelined, not resolved. Hamas's assault shattered the premise of a stable region anchored in Gulf-Israel cooperation: in its wake, the Saudi–Israeli deal collapsed, the Abraham Accords lost momentum, and IMEC—dependent on an "integrated Middle East"—became politically untenable. The "pivot to China" lay in ruins.

IF GAZA DERAILED the pivot, it also revealed—again—how much the Biden team had followed Trump's lead in the Middle East. Biden entered office promising to recalibrate relations with Saudi Arabia after American journalist Jamal Khashoggi was murdered in their Turkish embassy, to revive the Iran nuclear deal, and to "put human rights at the center" of U.S. foreign policy. By 2024 none of these goals were remotely on the agenda. Biden never engaged in meaningful nuclear negotiations; Saudi Prince Mohammed bin Salman, who allegedly called for Khashoggi's killing, was rehabilitated; and Washington underwrote what international organizations, human rights groups including in Israel, and legal and historical experts would broadly conclude was a genocide that left tens of thousands of Palestinians dead.

In the Middle East, Biden's only genuine commitment seemed to be to Israel, and so by extension the Abraham Accords. But the very states whose partnership in the Abraham Accords he had spent three years cultivating—the UAE, Bahrain, and Morocco—faced domestic backlash over Israel's war on Gaza; Saudi Arabia suspended talks; and Jordan and Egypt, longtime U.S. clients, publicly condemned Israeli actions. China, by contrast, used the moment to advertise itself as a mediator, hosting Arab delegations and amplifying calls for a Gaza ceasefire. Beijing's earlier success in brokering Saudi-Iranian rapprochement demonstrated its growing diplomatic reach. Now, it was leading an "Asia pivot" of its own.

By the time Biden shuffled off the campaign trail in July 2024, it was clear that every part of his elaborate plan had imploded. Israel's campaign in Gaza accelerated the drawdown of U.S. munitions stocks already depleted by Ukraine, forcing the Pentagon to stretch production lines meant for deterrence in the Pacific. Domestically, a Democratic base increasingly hostile to Israel eroded the political consensus needed for sustained competition with Beijing. And abroad, Gaza collapsed the moral clarity Biden had sought in framing a global contest between American democracy and Chinese autocracy. If anything, the images from Rafah and Khan Yunis seemed to invert just this legal and moral calculus for global audiences.

In his second term, Trump abandoned the Biden-era framing of U.S. power still in service of liberal internationalism. But Biden's actual practices in the Middle East—hard power, with few efforts at consensus-building, local legitimacy, or multilateral constraint—already demonstrated the extent to which Pax Americana was disintegrating. Trump 2.0 has now intensified these dynamics while doing away with surface narratives of democracy promotion, human rights, and the rule of law. In his recent speech at Davos, Canadian prime minister Mark Carney made just this point: the rules-based order has become little more than a fiction, and any stable multilateral order going forward cannot survive on grounds of the primacy of any single superpower—including the United States.

EVEN BEFORE TRUMP'S SECOND TERM, Washington's approach to Syria and Lebanon already exemplified what might best be described as primacy shorn of legitimacy. In late 2024, when the Syrian conflict turned in favor of domestic forces opposed to Assad's rule, Biden responded not by supporting reconstruction, but by encouraging Israeli attacks on post-Assad Syrian assets and sustaining sanctions that paralyzed the new government's economic recovery. The 2019 Caesar Act and related restrictions blocked access to banking systems and foreign investment, making it nearly impossible for Syrian institutions to rebuild even civilian infrastructure. Presented as leverage to promote "accountability," it left hospitals without fuel, municipalities without budgets, and refugees without prospects of return.

The interim Syrian government that formed early in the Trump administration pursued talks with Israel to end attacks, but was met with renewed coercion. Ongoing Israeli drone and missile strikes on southern Lebanon under the pretext of countering Hezbollah were extended eastward into southern Syria. Israel's conduct has been described as a "silent war" in the border provinces: targeted assassinations, precision strikes on infrastructure, and incursions into the 1974 demilitarized zone. By preventing Syria and Lebanon from restoring basic governance in their southern regions, Israel ensures a permanent security vacuum along its borders—a buffer not of peace, but of instability. Despite repealing the Caesar Act, Trump reinforced this logic through his own policies of coercive containment.

Likewise, the near-daily Israeli bombardments in southern Lebanon since 2024—sanctioned indirectly by Washington despite a purported more than year-old ceasefire—have devastated the area's infrastructure. Reports from the region chronicle how entire villages were razed under the rubric of "security operations," echoing campaigns in Gaza. The U.S. response has been to blame Hezbollah for the state's dysfunction, despite the fact that it has been effectively demobilized after Israel decapitated its leadership. In effect, Washington has abandoned Lebanese civil institutions while endorsing Israel's accelerating cross-border militarization. Instead of supporting reconstruction or political mediation, U.S. policy treats Lebanon as an extension of Israel's northern front—a territory to be disciplined rather than rebuilt.

Washington's "ironclad" commitment to Israel became the defining feature of its foreign policy and global posture.

This approach undermines not only Lebanon's sovereignty but also its fragile pluralism. By equating the Lebanese state with Hezbollah, U.S. officials conflate a confessional political system with a largely defeated militant movement, collapsing distinctions critical to Lebanese civilian governance. The result is a self-fulfilling prophecy: a "failed state," as U.S. envoy Thomas Barrack called it, whose fate has been ensured in part through external pressure. For Washington, the breakdown of Lebanese authority justifies giving Israel license for continued incursions—a license Israel then employs at will, even beyond these border regions. Following fears that the United States might intervene in Iran during Tehran's repression of mass popular protests, there is now speculation in the Israeli media that Tel Aviv might engage in such strikes, coordinated with the United States. The cycle of coercion sustains itself.

Combined, these policies perpetuate a zone of managed instability along and beyond Israel's northern and eastern borders. In Syria, the postwar transition becomes an externally managed process of containment, with "sovereignty" bounded by the interests of others. Worse still, the local experiment with self-determination in Syria's Kurdish region is now being extinguished. As part of its new security framework, the Trump administration is engaging in discretionary strikes on Syrian soil, purportedly against ISIS, but it has withdrawn support for the only force on the ground that had contained the Islamic State. In the process, the United States has licensed Damascus and Ankara to dismantle Kurdish self-governance in Rojava.

If Trump's foreign policy represents a rupture with Biden's, then the difference has hardly been felt by Syrians and Lebanese. Both administrations oversaw a bipartisan foreign policy consensus that authorized Israel to engage in constant military action. Both administrations refused to recognize the independent agency of communities in Lebanon and Syria. And both administrations have treated the region's recovery as a variable in their own strategic calculus: establishing a coercive architecture linking the Abraham Accords to the suppression of Iranian influence and the bolstering of Israeli regional military supremacy. Regardless of who governs in DC, American and Israeli preferences systematically override the sovereignty of local populations in the Middle East.

<hr>

TRUMP'S TWENTY-POINT Gaza ceasefire plan pursues this approach to its purest form: maximalist demands imposed through threats and incentives, bypassing local agency and real global buy-in alike. No Palestinian representatives of any kind, whether from Hamas or any other group across the political spectrum, were consulted in defining the "deal." The content of the proposal was more or less what Biden had previously proposed to Israel: a deal, he hoped, that would resuscitate the Abraham Accords while quieting domestic discontent about an ongoing genocide. Tel Aviv summarily rejected Biden's overtures, but under Trump, its posture has changed. Now, the Trump Administration can revive those Accords and enable potential Saudi participation in the United States's preferred regional architecture.

Trump gave Hamas what he called "three or four days" to comply with his plan, after which he promised to give Israel his "full backing to finish the job." The message was not subtle: accept the American-devised terms or face annihilation. This is diplomacy as a continuation of war by other means. The twenty-point plan imposes a technocratic administration—in no way chosen by Palestinians—under international supervision, with Trump allies reportedly responsible for oversight. The plan's terms in practice mean that the U.S. and Israel have sole discretion over whether civilians will be allowed access to real aid flows for relief and reconstruction—despite the clear human rights entitlements to these goods. And it makes that discretion dependent on whether Hamas capitulates by disarming and dissolving. In effect, Palestinians are presented with a form of ceasefire in which the experience of not being at imminent risk of death by bombardment is likely replaced by slow-motion killing via famine, disease, and exposure. At worst, cease-fire is twisted to mean merely a reduction (not a cessation) of ongoing Israeli bombardment.

Trump's demands may appear superficially reasonable to Western decisionmakers, who have long seen the rights of Gaza's Palestinians to the humanitarian prerequisites of their subsistence as conditional. In a world where Palestinians' human rights have become a bargaining chip, linking access to food, water and shelter to ultimatums is not new. But like so many Trump initiatives, the Gaza plan doubles down on American presumptions that force can substitute for legitimacy and that the weak will suffer what they must.

Of course, the plan's reliance on coercion is also its central weakness: it commands no genuine consent from those whose compliance it requires. The "stabilization" of Gaza is something to be enforced from without by "an international stabilization force," which third states have—no surprise—proven unwilling to join. By excluding Hamas, minimizing the role of the Palestinian Authority, and placing Gaza under foreign "trusteeship," the plan effectively and indefinitely blocks Palestinian self-determination. Palestinians are treated not as a community with legitimate political claims but as a problem to be managed and policed. There should be little shock, then, when this plan—like so many other diktats that preceded it—inevitably fails to generate either durable peace or stability: again, it refuses to address the enduring questions of occupation and self-determination driving the conflict.

The Gaza plan doubles down on American presumptions that force can substitute for legitimacy and that the weak will suffer what they must.

Internationally, the proposal undercuts the very norms that confer legitimacy on peacemaking. It was advanced without consultation with Palestinians but also by excluding the United Nations. The absence of a multilateral process was deliberate: Washington regards international institutions as obstacles rather than sources of authority. Under consistent criticism regionally and globally, the UN was eventually brought into the deal, but the belated imprimatur of the Security Council cannot legitimate it. The Gaza plan makes plain that the United Nations itself no longer serves as a forum to defend its founding commitments. Indeed, Trump's new "Board of Peace" is framed as a substitute for the United Nations, recasting the Gaza plan as a pilot for bypassing multilateral institutions he sees as constraining American leverage. More broadly, the Board institutionalizes his transactional worldview, built around ad-hoc bargaining forums calibrated to power, pressure, and dealmaking.

The familiar transactionalism of the Trump doctrine extends to the plan's economic proposals, which envision massive reconstruction projects and foreign investment once Gaza is "stabilized." The beneficiaries are conceived as America's allies in the region, awarded massive contracts and a captive territory in which to build experimental new projects. Leaked blueprints suggest that the Palestinians of Gaza will be pushed into makeshift dwellings on one half of the territory while the other half, depopulated and destroyed, will be the site for a bonanza of reconstruction grift stamped in the image of Trump's Gaza Riviera fantasy and possibly new Israeli settlements. Comments by IDF chief Eyal Zamir that the "yellow line" now dividing Gaza will constitute a "new border" for Israel makes clear that the partition is simply another vehicle for annexation. This is no Marshall Plan for Palestinians, to say the least, but effectively a fire sale of their land and resources.

<hr>

IN TRUMP'S BROADER CONCEPTION of global order, alliances are valued only insofar as they deliver immediate, tangible benefits. In this sense, the Gaza proposal mirrors his approach to NATO, trade policy, and negotiations with North Korea and Iran—high-stakes bargaining conducted through threats or extortion. What matters is not the infrastructure of peace and stability, let alone institutional legitimacy, but the optics of a "deal" struck by the world's strongest power complete with the promise of lucrative contracts.

Supporters of Trump's method argue that it produces results: hostages returned, rockets silenced, enemies cowed. Yet agreements reached under duress rarely survive the waning of coercive leverage. Already, "peace deals" Trump has touted in 2025, between Thailand and Cambodia, between Rwanda and the DRC, have begun to unravel as American attention has shifted elsewhere. Moreover, even the U.S.'s capacity to achieve ends through coercion alone has limits, as indicated by Trump's climbdown from demands to colonize Greenland.

China's greater diplomatic muscle—from brokering Saudi-Iranian rapprochement to backing ceasefire resolutions at the UN—and its deals struck with a range of counterparts, from Canada to the UAE, suggest that other actors understand rationally that they have to diversify their own portfolio of alliances. Likewise, the growing role of multilateral institutions under the auspices of alternative powers—whether the Shanghai Cooperation Organization or the increasing reliance on regional networks like Mercosur or ASEAN—may be less a consequence of other hegemons' ambitions than of how the American assault on its own post–World War II institutional order has left that order deeply compromised.

In this context, Trump has tended to punch down not up, avoiding direct confrontations with the United States' near-equivalent power players in China and Russia. Venezuela is a case in point: a far weaker adversary brought to heel through coercion. In the run-up to regime change in Caracas, the administration ratcheted up the pressure by carrying out extrajudicial killings, sanctioning and seizing oil tankers, and imposing a naval blockade—effectively trumpeting its pursuit of control from above in a bid to capture assets and establish a new client state.

Such a strategy closely mirrors the administration's longstanding playbook for the Middle East. In both cases, the Trump administration openly defends coercive intervention as a legitimate tool of statecraft, signals its intention to open post-transition economies to U.S. firms through lucrative reconstruction and extraction contracts, and frames military power as a means of securing reliable access to strategic resources—oil in particular, but also critical minerals. The administration's unwillingness to disengage from the Middle East is not only about security commitments or alliance politics, but also about treating the region as within the U.S. orbit and indispensable to global resource dominance. What emerges is a model of influence without legitimacy: power exercised through coercion, sanctions, and proxy governance rather than consent, law, or durable institutional buy-in. It's a worldview organized around regional spheres of influence and material control, in which the small players are subject to the whims of the powerful.

Of course, the United States has long leveraged its power to dominate weaker players and pursued Cold War objectives through extreme violence. But that violence was nonetheless in service of ideological ends that required it to actively build new multilateral institutions and invest significant material resources to "win hearts and minds." Now, however, documents like the NSS, along with gunboat diplomacy and annexation threats, appear in service of little beyond domination on grounds of "civilizational" superiority and might-makes-right asset expropriation. This fact is further driven home by the administration's series of travel bans, which embody its profound contempt for the idea of community with a world that is overwhelmingly Black and brown.

Under the Trump doctrine, the world is meant to be organized through regional hegemons that dictate the terms for their sphere of influence while maintaining their fortress walls. It speaks to the longstanding comfort Trump has had with dictators, including his openness to Saudi and Gulf influence (not to mention their money). In this way, the Trump doctrine depends on maintaining instrumental partnerships that are more stable in some ways (no grand conflagrations between the

United States and Russia or China, except maybe at the periphery), but pointedly less so in many others—especially for communities on the ground subject to extreme repression or arbitrary, capricious violence.

YET GAZA AND VENEZUELA also demonstrate—perhaps unintentionally—the intrinsic instability of such a coercive order. The Trump doctrine seeks control in a world that resists domination. By substituting coercion for consent, it multiplies the very crises it ostensibly aims to end. Not only does it underscore the degree to which the United States's global credibility has eroded; it demonstrates how pure coercion, in a context of real multipolar competition, is inevitably costlier and less effective at pursuing strategic ends.

In all the variations of American power since World War II, there is one approach that remains genuinely untested: multipolarity on inclusive terms, rather than through imperial rivalry. Such an approach would ground itself in the concerns of local publics and their own aspirations for self-determination. And it would link the domestic and foreign—from the Middle East to the streets of Minneapolis—through a vision of a world organized around mutual self-constraint, collective decision-making, and a shared global commons. Such meaningful self-determination, at home and abroad, has always been the only plausible pathway to a more just and stable future. But for now, Palestine, Venezuela, Lebanon, and Syria stand as stark embodiments of that pathway's continued foreclosure. **BR**

THE CRYPTO CHOKEHOLD

Gerald Epstein

WITHOUT DONALD TRUMP, the crypto industry would have met a very different fate. In the years before his second presidential campaign kicked off, crypto markets were undergoing a series of downturns that, if not necessarily spelling cryptocurrency's death knell, were threatening to dramatically weaken the standing of an asset class that had minted a new generation of economic elites, relegating it to the status of a niche object for the likes of tech hobbyists, online gamblers, and drug dealers. 2022 in particular was such a bad time for crypto that commentators started to refer to it as a "crypto winter." The value of Bitcoin—the cryptocurrency that, back in 2009, gave birth to the crypto revolution in the first place—had skyrocketed in the few preceding years, but in November 2022 it fell precipitously, taking down many crypto initiates with it. Sam Bankman-Fried's FTX, at its peak the third-largest crypto exchange in the world, collapsed, and Bankman-Fried and his friends were arrested. Apart from the most enthusiastic keepers of the faith, few were predicting a turnaround anytime soon.

But by the fall of 2025, crypto was booming again. The value of Bitcoin grew sixfold, from its 2023 trough of $20,000 up to $120,000, with the total value of crypto assets more than tripling in the same period. In the year leading up to June 2025, the number of crypto billionaires grew by almost a third, reaching thirty-six people. And Trump, who had spent much of the campaign trail promising to keep the good times rolling, rode those rising tides all the way to the White House.

At one point, the President might have seemed an unlikely savior. During his first term and after leaving office, he was a vocal skeptic, denouncing crypto as a "scam" and warning that it could undermine the U.S. dollar. But by 2024, Trump announced that he was the crypto candidate—and, if elected, would make the United States the "crypto capital of the planet." His conversion was the culmination of a long-term crypto lobbying campaign—with its promise of significant political donations—and, even more importantly, his awakening to the possibilities of personal enrichment for an otherwise cash-strapped Trump family enterprise.

For the crypto industry, Trump was only one target of their intense, highly focused intervention into the 2024 elections. By some estimates, crypto firms spent over $245 million, more than any other industry. Leading the charge were three major pro-crypto PACs—Fairshake, Protect Progress, and Defend American Jobs—which raised and channeled funds from firms like Coinbase, Ripple, and Jump Crypto and investors like Andreessen Horowitz and the Winklevoss twins (Tyler and Cameron) to elect as broad a bipartisan slate of pro-crypto candidates as possible.

It was an astonishingly successful effort. The PACs spent $40 million to defeat Democrat Sherrod Brown in Ohio and elect his Republican challenger, but they also supported pro-crypto Democrats Elissa Slotkin in Michigan and Ruben Gallego in Arizona, among others. They spent over $10 million in California to defeat crypto critic Katie Porter in a Senate primary against the more pro-crypto Democrat Adam Schiff, and they spent more than $2 million against Jamaal Bowman, a New York Democrat who had denounced crypto. After Bowman's defeat, Tyler Winklevoss took to X with a warning: "Politicians everywhere need to understand that this is what happens when you pick a fight with the crypto army." He had reason to gloat: of the 58 House and Senate races Fairshake entered, their favored candidate won in 53 of them. As the dust settled on the 2024 election, Winklevoss and the other major crypto players would find their interests now thoroughly represented throughout the federal government.

Of course, their biggest win was in making an avid crypto fan out of President Trump, who, once in office, wasted little time repaying his donors' largesse. In February he appointed a swath of pro-crypto officials to run major financial regulatory agencies: Paul Atkins as Chair of the Securities and Exchange Commission (SEC), Scott Bessent as Treasury Secretary, Jonathan Gould as comptroller of the currency. And he created a whole new position, "AI and crypto czar," to which he appointed David Sacks—who, in his first press conference, would declare triumphantly that "the war on crypto is over."

At this point it should be clear that the speed, scope, and scale of crypto's rise from the ashes reflects the success of a political project much more than a purely economic one. But just what does this project seek to accomplish—and at whose cost? By harnessing the greed and corruption of the Trump family and its cronies, as well as many Democrats, the crypto industry has assembled a juggernaut of power that aims to revolutionize the financial system to place crypto and their businesses at the center of finance, not just in the United States but throughout the globe. The most immediate economic risk of this is the prospect of a crypto-induced financial crisis—a danger exacerbated by the industry's ever-tighter entanglement with the looming AI bubble.

But Trump and his tech-sector allies do not plan to stop there. Not only do they want to take over the private financial system; they also want to privatize the most important public financial asset in the world economy: the U.S. dollar. By tying crypto to the dollar through so-called stablecoins, they hope to reap the rewards accruing to the United States by the singular role its currency plays in the global economy—a project whose success depends on Trump's political power, the continuous (and increasing) support of the U.S. Treasury and Federal Reserve, and a barrage of deregulation to clear the way.

FOR NOW, TRUMP and his family are happy enough to use their ties to the crypto industry as a moneymaking venture. Through the release of the $TRUMP and $MELANIA memecoins and a large stake in World Liberty Financial, a crypto-connected financial enterprise founded by Trump and his Middle East envoy, Steve Witkoff, the Trump family has increased its wealth by billions (exact estimates vary). In August, *New Yorker* staff writer David D. Kirkpatrick estimated judiciously that 70 percent of the $3.4 billion the Trump family has made from exploiting Donald Trump's role as president so far has come from crypto-related ventures. Much of the finance inflow has come from abroad.

For many crypto titans, the real value in such investments lies in the access to the Trump family and the favors it makes possible. A case in point is the set of deals the Trump family made with the United Arab Emirates (UAE). Last January, it agreed to sell a 49 percent stake in World Liberty Financial to an Abu Dhabi sheikh for nearly half a billion dollars. Months later, a government-backed firm in the UAE bought $2 billion using cryptocurrency offered by World Liberty Financial, while Witkoff negotiated the selling of highly advanced computer chips to the UAE government at the same time. Together, the deals allowed a foreign government to forge extraordinarily close ties to the president—and generated hundreds of millions of dollars for the Trumps and their associates.

The speed, scope, and scale of crypto's rise from the ashes reflects the success of a political project much more than a purely economic one.

Playing a major role in the latter deal's financing was Changpeng Zhao, perhaps the world's richest crypto capitalist and the main owner of Binance, perhaps the largest crypto trading platform. Prosecuted during the Biden administration for money laundering to terrorist groups (among others), Zhao served four months in prison and stepped down as chair of Binance in 2023. But in October, Trump pardoned Zhao, leaving him free to retake management control of Binance—and, evidently, to join team Trump.

Given the growing roster of crypto titans he now counts as allies, it's little surprise that Trump, upon taking office, introduced a sweeping set of deregulatory measures designed to take the heat off of them. In February, Trump signed an executive order "pausing" enforcement of the Foreign Corrupt Practices Act for 180 days. In April, the administration disbanded the Department of Justice's (DOJ) entire National Crypto Enforcement Team. That same month, the DOJ would issue a memo announcing it would no longer investigate or bring money laundering or illicit finance cases against trading platforms, digital wallets, or anonymity-boosting services known as mixers and tumblers. And the SEC, now in the hands of Trump loyalists, slashed its crypto enforcement staff and dropped investigations and lawsuits—especially against crypto companies that had direct ties to the Trump family.

———

DESPITE BEING CALLED a currency, crypto lacks one of the most important characteristics that a currency should have: a stable value. Cryptocurrencies have proved far more unstable than other financial assets and certainly more unpredictable than the value of the dollar, which has fallen in recent years by 2 to 3 percent a year (the rate of inflation). Admittedly, most of crypto's fluctuations have not reached hyperinflation extremes, but some cryptocurrencies have completely collapsed in value (in fact, according to one estimate, more than 50 percent of them have failed since 2021). For those who want to expand the use of cryptocurrencies, such volatility poses serious problems. Enter stablecoins, assets that are designed, as the name suggests, to hold a stable value by tying their values to that of another important asset, such as the U.S. dollar. If successfully locked in one-to-one with the U.S. dollar, stablecoins would only vary to the same degree as the dollar does. First and foremost, stablecoins promise to expand the market for crypto assets and enhance profits for those who own them.

What can go wrong? The answer partly depends on how well stablecoins are regulated and by whom. That's where the GENIUS Act (short for "Guiding and Establishing National Innovation for U.S. Stablecoins Act") comes in. It was signed into law by President Trump in July, after passing the Senate with 50 Republican and 18 Democratic votes and the House with 206 Republican and 102 Democratic votes. The act provides a highly permissive legal framework for wannabe stablecoin purveyors by allowing both banks and non-banks to issue stablecoins: now, JPMorgan Chase, asset managers like BlackRock and Fidelity, and even non-financial corporations like Amazon or Walmart can all issue them.

When you put $100 into your checking account, you have the right to withdraw your dollars on demand, and the bank is required to give them to you: banks are required to have deposit insurance so that if there is a run, you can still get your money back. They are also required to keep a certain amount of capital on hand, so that if they lose money, its owners still must pay up. Regulatory rules limit the types of assets banks can invest in, to discourage high-risk investments. The GENIUS Act imposes none of these rules on institutions that issue stablecoins. It prohibits them from paying interest on deposits, in order to protect traditional banks from competition, but it also allows them to get around these restrictions by offering rewards—so deposits are likely to flee from banks subject to regulations and safeguards to crypto purveyors that aren't.

It is unclear how successful these purveyors will be in maintaining stable links to the dollar, but history suggests the likelihood of serious problems. Economic historian Barry Eichengreen documented how chaos ensued when local banks issued their own currencies in the mid-nineteenth century, the period sometimes referred to as the "wildcat banking" era. Back then, shopkeepers and farmers had a hard time determining which currency was stable and which was not, because bank runs were so common. As a result, the Lincoln administration enacted several laws to place the national banking system under stricter regulation.

Today, we are inching closer and closer to the wildcat days. Some stablecoins, such as Tether, have been pushed off their pegs to the dollar multiple times, leading to a collapse in the cryptocurrency's value. The 2023 bank runs on Silicon Valley Bank, Signature Bank, and Silvergate Bank were partly the result of their ties to the crypto industry. Although the GENIUS Act purports to avoid these problems by requiring stablecoin issuers to keep high-quality assets such as short-term U.S. Treasury securities on hand to guarantee deposits, they have every incentive to cheat. Holding safe assets earns them very low returns; if they can take some of the investments and buy riskier assets, they can earn a lot more money. We have every reason to believe that this is what they will do.

Joining the GENIUS Act is the Clarity Act, which has passed the House and is awaiting approval by the Senate. If signed into law, the legislation will lead to the near-total deregulation of crypto, gutting almost all financial regulations and monitoring mechanisms that could place limits on the system. At the same time, as a law, it creates a patina of legitimacy for "whatever goes" finance. The coalition group Americans for Financial Reform has mobilized efforts to fight this bill, which would surely usher in a new era of consumer abuse and financial instability, but as of this writing, the act is closer than ever to passing. And even if it does not pass, the GENIUS Act, combined with the administrative decisions made by the now firmly pro-crypto financial regulators, are enough to tear down the guardrails on their own.

THE ROSTER OF Trump supporters with much to gain from crypto is a who's who of tech and finance capitalists. These include the usual suspects: the so-called "PayPal mafia," billionaires who got their start with PayPal, notably Peter Thiel and David Sacks; Marc Andreessen of Andreessen Horowitz, a former Democratic supporter turned Trump fundraiser; and Zhao, perhaps the wealthiest crypto maven in the world. But they also include a host of no less powerful people who like to fly further under the radar: Brian Armstrong, Co-founder and CEO of Coinbase; Justin Sun, the crypto entrepreneur and top investor in the $TRUMP coin; and Michael Saylor, the billionaire who has supported Trump's plans to create a national Bitcoin reserve.

Over the past year, most of these allies have enjoyed the free-dom—and lucrative returns—brought on by the new (de)regulatory environment. But some, it appears, are thinking even bigger: a fever dream to turn the libertarian vision of decentralized finance without government on its head by privatizing and taking over the financial system in as much of the world as they can. This is no classic libertarian vision of "free banking," which wants the system completely privatized without government backing. On the contrary, their vision is that, at least initially, this system will be anchored by the U.S. dollar, and that the government and Federal Reserve will stand behind it, subsidize it, and if necessary, bail it out when it gets in trouble. To do so, they plan to control the system from within by creating an unregulated parallel system based on cryptocurrencies and assets, and allowing—indeed encouraging—banks and other "legacy" financial institutions to inte-grate them into their overall operations to avoid being outcompeted by new crypto-focused ones.

Stablecoins, the GENIUS Act, and deregulatory decisions at the major financial regulatory agencies like the SEC are at this program's leading edge. Soon, the injection of crypto into our current financial system via stablecoins and other products, writes Aaron Krolik of the *New York Times*, may unknowingly involve everyday users of banking, credit cards, saving, and investing. As Timothy Massad, who served as the Treasury Assistant Secretary for financial stability after the 2008 crash, put it: "The line between betting, speculating and investing has largely disappeared." (Such matters, it turns out, also worried John Maynard Keynes with respect to Wall Street in the run-up to the 1929 crash.)

The ever-tightening crypto chokehold heralds both the naked extraction of more wealth by a relatively few capitalists and the severe risk of a massive financial crisis.

This ever-tightening crypto chokehold heralds a number of problems. One, of course, is the naked extraction of more wealth by a relatively few wealthy cryptocapitalists, especially those with ties to Trump and his family. The other is a severe risk of a massive financial crisis—not only because of the same risks of deregulation that caused the 1930s and 2008 breakdowns, but because, as economist Hélène Rey points out, crypto is subject to hacking and manipulation that could cause a situation to spiral further out of control.

What are the prospects for a crash? Typically, risk is high when the value of financial assets is inflated or volatile. In trying to determine the values of financial assets such as the price of Apple or Ford Motor stocks, mainstream economists focus on what they call "fundamentals," the profits that can be reasonably expected a company will earn over the foreseeable future. If buying a share of stock makes one a partial owner of a company and entitles them to that share of the company's profits, then it makes sense to think of reasonably expected future profits as a fundamental determinant of the price a stock owner would be willing to pay for a share. A related determinant is risk: if the uncertainty surrounding the forecast of future profits is high, then investors might be willing to pay somewhat less for their slice of expected future profits.

But as Keynes has pointed out, in many common circumstances, these fundamentals are not even close to being strong enough to nail down equity prices. For one, there can be considerable uncertainty about a company's future profitability, especially if the overall economy is uncertain, or if the company or product is new and untested. A second, related reason, according to Keynes, paradoxically, has to do with the ease with which investors can buy and sell stocks—what economists sometimes call the "liquidity" of stock markets. If investors have a lot of uncertainty about future fundamentals, they can still make money by just following the investor crowd's gossip and rumors. If the crowd believes that other investors are going to buy an asset because it is getting hyped by the President of the United States, then they will buy it too. If they start sensing news that "the markets" are turning sour on a stock, they might try to get ahead of the markets and dump it. In a world of great uncertainty and high liquidity that makes it easy to buy and sell, short-term guesses and rumors rather than longer term fundamentals will rule investor behavior.

Crypto, of course, is an asset ripe for hype and rumor. Because it does not work as a medium of exchange (like actual money), or generate a rate of return (because it generates no income), its value stems from its utility in skirting the law—tax evasion, buying and selling illegal products, and the like—and as a vehicle for speculation on its own ups and downs. In the latter case, its value is determined almost entirely by how much hype people believe that other people believe, even if they don't believe it themselves.

MIT economic historian Charles Kindleberger and his colleagues, Robert Aliber and Robert N. McCauley, have developed a framework of financial "manias, panics, and crashes" that is useful for understanding crypto's fluctuations. Some crises, they argue, involve speculative bubbles followed by crashes, like the Dutch tulip bubble of the 1600s or the real estate sub-prime bubble of the mid-2000s. In each case, the bubbles exhibit a characteristic pattern: first, there is an initial exogenous event, or *displacement*, that sets off an asset price rise, which gathers momentum and becomes a *boom*. As the boom continues, investors begin to check their reason and caution at the door. *Euphoria*, or what Alan Greenspan called "irrational exuberance," takes hold. Then some investors begin to see weakness in the boom and start selling in an increasing wave of *profit taking*; as profit taking takes hold, investors run for the exits as panic selling—often at a loss—takes over.

Crypto's recent history is a case study. In late 2024, *displacement* started moving crypto prices up. Momentum soon accumulated into a *boom* as the Trump family and allies made more crypto deals, created a federal "crypto reserve," directed their financial regulators to ease restrictions on crypto, and ultimately passed legislation to create a "non-regulatory" set of regulations for crypto. Boom soon led to *euphoria* as crypto prices started climbing into the stratosphere. By late October 2025, *profit taking* creeped in and prices started to fall dramatically, in a nosedive from which it has not recovered.

The overall size, growth rate, and destructiveness of these bubbles—both on the way up and on the way down—is much greater if they are fueled by leverage. If you pay $100 for an asset, but borrow $80 to buy it (so you only put $20 of your own wealth into it), if the price of the asset drops by just 50 percent ($50) then you not only lose your whole investment, but you have to come up with $30 someplace else to repay your debt. In a 2024 study, the Federal Reserve Bank of New York warned of crypto's risks to financial instability, including problems with excessive leverage. They highlighted crypto firms advertising debt-to-asset ratios of one hundred, a highly significant level of leverage. Crypto bets in derivatives, they pointed out, also involve high risks that amount to high leverage, because small bets can lead to large gains or losses—and the latter often have to be made up by selling other assets. (The downturn is further made worse if there is a lack of clarity in the market as to where the skeletons are buried: which institutions are holding bad assets, how much have they borrowed to buy these assets, who have they borrowed from—and who might not get paid if the bubble crashes.) In other words, leverage, interconnectedness, and transparency determine the amount of collateral damage from a bubble crash—and the crypto economy is at once leveraged, interconnected, and exceedingly opaque.

Because crypto does not have any intrinsic value, its value could fall very far—indeed, all the way to zero, as has happened with many cryptocurrencies. But if the government is committed to bailing out (putting a floor under) the value of some crypto assets, that will embolden private investors to buy. That Donald Trump and his family are now major crypto investors almost certainly suggests to other investors that his administration would never let the values of these assets collapse. Were such a bailout to take place, the big investors would keep their money while the economy around them is steadily drained.

MULTIPLYING THE DANGERS from crypto is the fact that it is expanding in an economy increasingly dominated by another very risky technology: artificial intelligence. The AI equity bubble and data center building spree, increasingly financed by risky transactions, creates an independent vector of economic, financial, and environmental risk in the U.S. economy. Not only can crypto risks can be exacerbated by the risks associated with AI; crypto can also increase AI's dangers at the same time.

Instead of leading the opposition to Trump's crypto plans, many prominent Democrats have stood meekly by—or worse, encouraged them.

The clearest connection between the two industries is in their compounding of environmental risks. Server farms associated with crypto mining piled on top of massive computer data centers being built by AI companies dramatically worsen the environmental problems of fossil fuel use, water shortages, land scarring, and community disruption. But there are other emerging interactive threats, too. Generally, crypto asset prices are highly correlated with the stock market (by some measures, in fact, crypto prices *over*-react to changes in the stock market). Today, we seem to be experiencing not only a bubble in crypto asset prices but also a bubble in AI-related equity prices, especially in the prices of the so-called "Magnificent Seven" companies that dominate the stock market: Alphabet (Google), Amazon, Apple, Meta (Facebook), Microsoft, Nvidia, and Tesla, whose stocks now account for about a third of the total value of the stock exchange. If these stocks were to precipitously decline in value, then so too would crypto—potentially leading to a two-headed crisis in both the traditional and crypto markets.

The financial system is becoming increasingly fragile because of deregulation, increased leverage, and reduced transparency. All this implies that a shock to one part of the system—for example, the equity values of the "Magnificent Seven"—is more likely to have unpredictable and serious negative knock-on effects elsewhere.

But perhaps the biggest danger of the interaction between crypto and AI is the political connection between the two. Under the tenure of their newly purchased champion Donald Trump, the techno-industrial elite—or as political scientist Thomas Ferguson calls them, "red tech"—have become dangerously powerful. A glance at the high-tech billionaires who attended Trump's inauguration gives one window into this bloc: Mark Zuckerberg (Meta), Elon Musk (Tesla, X), Jeff Bezos (Amazon), Sundar Pichai (Google) and Tim Cook (Apple). Add to that list the investors behind the crypto PACs, and, as Ferguson rightly points out, military contractors and oil and gas executives, and one gets a full picture of the coalition feeding the Republicans, many Democrats, and, of course, Trump himself.

Especially now that this bloc's reach extends to a number of key congressional Democrats, there is an increasingly high likelihood for a government bailout of both crypto and AI, should their connected bubbles burst. Indeed, we have already witnessed some take place. In November, Bessent and the Trump administration promised to lend up to $20 billion to Javier Milei in Argentina to help him win re-election, partly because of failed financial bets made by U.S. hedge funds in Argentina. And in December, Trump pumped up AI values by issuing an executive order to try to prevent states from regulating the technology themselves.

WHILE THE CRYPTO and AI madness is at the leading edge of the economic insanity stalking the country, it is only the most visible symptom of a deeply destructive political bloc taking control over our politics. Bringing sanity to the asylum is no simple task, but the fact that we are teetering on the precipice of a highly probable financial crash ought to focus our attention on doing so. Trump and his allies figure that they can push the system as hard as it can go, and if it cracks, the government can just bail them (if not the economy) out. In the meantime, they will continue to privatize and take control over the monetary and financial system.

A three-pronged strategy could, in principle, prevent this. First would be to restore financial regulations to prevent the unchecked spread of crypto and stablecoins into the financial system. This would require repealing the GENIUS Act, restoring financial stability-based perspectives on crypto at the SEC and other regulatory agencies, restoring money laundering and fraud prosecutions by the Justice Department, and reaffirming the financial stability rules embodied in the Dodd-Frank Act, imperfect as these are.

Second would be to reinforce support for public digital payments systems, including those outlawed by the GENIUS Act. And third: no bailouts for the crypto and AI capitalists at the expense of the rest of the country. When the crypto bubble bursts, the Federal Reserve and Treasury should keep the payments systems working, protect people's savings, and keep employment humming by using fiscal support if necessary, as it did during the COVID shutdown. But above all, make the tech broligarchy take the hit.

Still, an unsettling question looms: Is there sufficient political will to accomplish any of this? Instead of leading the opposition to Trump's crypto plans, many prominent Democrats have stood meekly by—or worse, encouraged them. In the meantime, the crypto money that wracked the 2024 contests is worming its way into the next cycle. Recent reports show that crypto interests are amassing more than $250 million for the 2026 elections to get even more pro-crypto candidates nominated and elected to Congress while driving out the candidates standing in their way. Increasingly, they are focusing on Democratic primary races, and even state-level Democratic committees, in an attempt to insulate themselves from the effects of a possible Republican defeat.

Within the party, there is a battle raging between progressive, anti-crypto Democrats—like Representatives Alexandria Ocasio-Cortez and Pramila Jayapal and Senators Elizabeth Warren and Bernie Sanders—and the corporate, pro-crypto wing led by Senator Chuck

Schumer. Joining the former in their fight against the crypto takeover are reform groups like Americans for Financial Reform and Better Markets, who have mobilized supporters to sign on to letters, lobby, and demonstrate. Yet as long as the new wave of Democrats allied to the crypto industry continues to gain a foothold in the party, it will be an uphill battle. **BR**

Senator Chuck Schumer conducts a news conference in the U.S. Capitol in May 2025. Image: AP

HOW NOT TO DEFEAT AUTHORITARIANISM

Adam Bonica & Jake Grumbach

This essay opens a large debate on the future of the Democratic Party. Read responses—by Cori Bush, Suzanne Mettler, Matthew Yglesias, Eric Rauchway, and many others—on our website.

IN 2024, **DEMOCRACY WAS** "on the ballot." That, at any rate, was the popular slogan. To which there was a popular response: Democrats must moderate! "Moderation" was the key to winning elections, it was said, and winning elections was the only way to turn back the existential threat to democracy.

If you watched on Election Night expecting Kamala Harris's appeals to moderates would pay off, only to see them fall short, you weren't alone. Political consultants bet heavily on the same calculation. Harris distanced herself from progressive positions (including some she herself had previously supported), emphasized kitchen-table issues, and courted Liz Cheney. She lost anyway.

But the idea that moderation is the path to victory—and thus to preserving democracy—remains a matter of firm conviction among many political commentators and consultants. The *New York Times* editorial board recently declared that "moving to the center is the way to win," dismissing research that finds otherwise as lost in "statistical complexities." As prominent pundit Matthew Yglesias wrote in early 2025, "What the Democrats need . . . is not just more moderate candidates. They need a more moderate ideology." Or, in political scientist Ruy Teixeira's words from 2022, "Moderation = Democratic votes." On this view, the primary reason that Democrats are losing is that voters perceive the national party as too extreme: embracing policy positions or activist groups on issues that too many people see as too far from the mainstream, from policing and climate change to immigration and transgender rights. And Harris's efforts to repair those perceptions were too little, too late.

There are many dissenting voices. Zohran Mamdani, for one, warned against bowing "at the altar of caution" in his victory speech in November. But the *Times*, Yglesias, and Teixeira are hardly alone in preaching at this altar. And as proponents of moderation will be quick to say, Mamdani won in New York City, not the swing districts in California's Central Valley and Pennsylvania's suburbs that a national party needs to win real governing power, from the presidency to the Senate. Moderation, in short, remains the conventional political wisdom.

We think this view is wrong. In an era of intense partisanship, nationalized elections, and low trust in elites and institutions, the electoral benefits of moderation are at best small and inconsistent, at worst counterproductive—in any case, not a reliable path to electoral victory or to meeting the existential threats to democracy. Moderation is more

conventional than wise, and the most prominent cases for it badly mis-
understand how politics works.

WHY DO SO MANY think moderation is the right way to win? The most
familiar and intuitive argument is that it's simply what voters say they
want. This view is strongly associated with *popularism*, a way of thinking
about politics that has flourished in Democratic circles since 2020.

Popularists argue that candidates who want to win elections need
to focus relentlessly on what polls well and abandon what doesn't. The
claim is not that progressive policies and progressive rhetoric are bad on
the merits, though popularists do sometimes criticize them on this basis.
The claim is that too many voters are turned off by progressive ideas,
dooming Democrats' chances to win office *and* pursue any agenda to
the left of the GOP. Popularism's strategic imperative is thus framed as a
hardheaded corrective to progressive idealism.

Ezra Klein has summarized the view this way: "Democrats should do
a lot of polling to figure out which of their views are popular and which are
not popular, and then they should talk about the popular stuff and shut
up about the unpopular stuff." The job of a campaign, in other words,
is to discover what voters already want and package it for sale. To win
elections, Democrats need to treat voters as consumers with fixed preferences, not as citizens whose behavior is malleable and whose views are
responsive to media, leadership, and persuasion.

This approach to politics is not new. The technical term is political
pandering, and it is as old as democracy itself. Thucydides derided the
Athenian demagogue Cleon as a leader guided not by wisdom but by
whatever drew the assembly's loudest applause. Political theorists have
long treated Cleon as a warning: when leaders stop leading and instead
mirror the crowd, democratic institutions decay. Popularism cloaks this
same impulse in empiricism. The roar of the crowd has been replaced
by polling data, but the emptiness remains. Worse, Cleon's pandering
at least stirred the crowd. The moderation that popularists recommend
dampens enthusiasm, demobilizes or even alienates the base, and cedes
the affective terrain to opponents who are happy to rile people up.

To be fair, popularism does correctly diagnose a bind that Democrats face. They are geographically concentrated in ways that create structural disadvantages in the Senate and Electoral College; in order to win a governing majority, they need to do well among relatively conservative districts and can't afford to alienate most voters outside deep-blue urban areas. But popularism's prescription is fatally limited. It confuses listening with leadership and measurement with meaning, assuming that elections are won by calibrating positions to match local preferences.

Political scientists Christopher Achen and Larry Bartels systematically rebutted this assumption—and the more general folk theory that people mainly vote on the basis of freestanding policy preferences—in their 2016 book *Democracy for Realists*. Moreover, as Daniel Hopkins shows in *The Increasingly United States* (2018), contemporary U.S. politics are more nationalized and polarized than ever—trends that render preference-matching efforts especially ineffective. Tip O'Neill, Speaker of the House from 1977 to 1987, urged that "all politics is local." That's not true anymore. Elections have become national referendums, less impacted by candidates' stated policy positions. Even the most finely tuned messaging is being drowned out by partisan tides. In short, it is much harder for candidates to outrun their party than it once was.

More fundamentally, the popularist fixation on polls undermines the movement energy required to confront authoritarian threats. Popularists see voters as fixed points—or at least extremely rigid ones—instead of as agents whose preferences can be mobilized and transformed. But in moments of democratic crisis, politics is a search for the right movement, not the right maneuver. Playing defense forfeits the moral clarity and collective purpose that have sustained successful anti-authoritarian movements worldwide.

SO MUCH FOR the wisdom of chasing polls. But can a case for moderation be made independently of the argument for pandering? Here, too, the popularist refrain contains a grain of truth. For decades, the electoral benefits of moderation were real and well-documented. Political scientists developed rigorous tools to measure candidate ideology and found that centrist candidates often outperformed their more ideological counterparts. Claims that moderation helped win votes had empirical support.

But that was a different era. As elections nationalized and polarization intensified, the old rules stopped applying. A growing body of research now demonstrates that the moderation advantage has largely disappeared. In the Trump era, candidate ideology has little consistent effect on vote share. The scholarly consensus has shifted. The popularist case for moderation has not kept up. Instead, it relies on analyses that ignore this research.

While democracy faces an existential threat, pundits and strategists remain stuck in the past.

Perhaps the most prominent metric comes from Split Ticket, an organization of political data analysts that claims moderates dramatically outperform progressives. Their metric, called Wins Above Replacement (WAR), is borrowed from baseball, estimating how much a player contributes to a team's success compared to a replacement-level alternative. In that context, WAR can provide some insight because each player generates data from over a hundred games per season. A congressional candidate, by contrast, faces voters once every two years. As political scientist and statistician Andrew Gelman has noted, this means political WAR estimates are far more uncertain and should not be taken too seriously.

Moreover, Split Ticket's analysis is proprietary; the group does not disclose how it calculates estimates, so the assumptions built into its model cannot be independently evaluated. When we tested the group's metric against a transparent baseline—how well a candidate performed relative to their party's presidential nominee—we found that less than a third of Split Ticket's WAR score reflected actual candidate overperformance; the rest came from undisclosed adjustments. We tried to replicate Split Ticket's results, testing dozens of reasonable modeling approaches and different measures of ideology. None produced effects anywhere near as large. Other analyses, including data journalist G. Elliott Morris's transparent and replicable WAR model, reached similar conclusions. Morris's verdict echoes our own: moderation is "overrated" and "not a silver bullet."

The *Times* editorial board recently made a case similar to Split Ticket's on the basis of PAC endorsements, comparing candidates backed by centrist PACs against everyone else—including unfunded candidates in hopeless races. This comparison just doesn't make sense. If you apply the same method to candidates backed by progressive PACs, you find that they *also* appear to outperform everyone else until you adjust for fundraising and incumbency, in which case the apparent advantage again vanishes. The *Times* dismissed academic research as too complex and disconnected from voter perceptions, yet when we measure ideology based on how voters perceive candidates, the moderation effect is the smallest of any measure tested.

At a fundamental level, both Split Ticket's analysis and the *Times*'s confuse correlation with causation. Joe Manchin is the poster child for moderation's supposed benefits, but his success reflects decades of personal brand-building in a state that realigned around him. His moderation was credible to West Virginia voters in a way a replacement Democrat's would not be. Indeed, when Manchin retired and Democrats nominated Glenn Elliott, also a moderate, Elliott lost by 40 points. The lesson isn't that moderation wins; it's that being Manchin wins.

To illuminate the analytical challenges underlying these debates, consider a simple, transparent metric: how much better or worse a congressional candidate performs compared to their party's presidential nominee in the same district. Being an incumbent generally provides a substantial electoral boost of 2 to 3 percentage points above the presidential nominee's performance; in contrast, shifting dramatically to the ideological center yields at most negligible benefits. (We get the same result no matter how we measure candidate ideology.)

Political scientists have developed approaches that get beyond the correlations that plague popularist models. We have used these approaches to test whether moderation wins elections. We built a comprehensive measure of ideology by combining over a dozen distinct metrics—from congressional voting records and campaign finance data to the policy positions on candidate websites to voter evaluations. And we employed research designs that can distinguish causal effects from correlations. For example, we looked at very closely contested Democratic primaries that included both a moderate and a progressive candidate. Because the primaries are so closely contested, the winner is essentially random, as if someone flipped a coin to determine which candidate would get the nomination. (This research design ensures that we're studying the effect of moderation independent of all other factors, such as whether the district was red, blue, or purple.) We then considered whether the moderates who won these coin-flip primaries did better in the general election than the progressives who won them. They didn't.

Playing defense forfeits the moral clarity and collective purpose that have powered successful anti-authoritarian movements worldwide.

Putting all this together, the results are clear. Moderation *used* to help candidates in past decades, but in the Trump era, a candidate's ideological moderation has no consistent, measurable effect on their vote share. Moderation as a strategy hit its ceiling in 2024. With moderates already dominating the battlefield in every competitive district, the potential gains from moving further to the center were exhausted. Still, Democrats made their wager: from the presidential nominee down to local candidates, they fully deployed the popularist strategy of moderate, "kitchen table" messaging. The result? A Republican trifecta. The party bet on moderation, but the strategy, on its own, proved unable to meet the moment. The record of who actually wins and loses reinforces the point. Of the 22 Democratic incumbents who lost competitive seats between 2016 and 2024, 21 were moderates. Only one was a progressive.

We are not alone in these findings. A number of recent scholarly studies converge on a theoretically interesting and practically important conclusion: yes, moderation was once a powerful force in U.S. politics, but its effects have shrunk to the point of (at most) being small and highly context-dependent. A small moderation bonus may exist in some contexts, but it has nowhere near the campaign-defining effect its boosters claim. In the Trump era, moderation has no consistent, measurable effect on vote share. Whatever small advantage once existed has been exhausted, and with moderates already running in nearly every competitive district, there are no more gains to be had. The strategy has been fully deployed. It has not delivered.

This raises a pair of key questions. What has changed? And what has taken the place of the old rules?

————————————————

TO BEGIN TO ANSWER, it helps to step back from election statistics and think about the substance of modern American politics.

One of political science's most elegant theories offers a starting point: the *median voter theorem.* It was given expression in Anthony Downs's 1957 book, *An Economic Theory of Democracy.* Imagine voters arranged along a line from left to right. The median voter sits in the middle, with half the electorate to the left, half to the right. If candidate Jones moves away from the middle to the left, they will lose the voters who are now closer to candidate Smith, and not gain anything because the voters further to the left were already going to vote for Jones. Like ice cream vendors setting up in the center of a beach, candidates should rationally move toward that midpoint to win the most votes.

The model is very simple and, for decades, it worked. In the 1980s and 1990s, moderates often outperformed their parties. But that advantage has eroded for structural reasons.

First, who the median voter is depends on who shows up to vote. When turnout among younger and more diverse voters surges, the median shifts left; when it's low, older and more conservative voters pull it right. The strategic question isn't just how to appeal to the median voter, but how to build an electorate that generates a median voter favorable to your goals. So the popularist focus on persuading a small number of swing voters is misplaced: that focus may dampen turnout and shift the median voter to the right.

In contemporary elections, what really matters is which party gets more of its voters to the polls. The turnout gap between Democrats and Republicans is a powerful predictor of election outcomes. As the data show, Democratic national vote share rises and falls with their ability to close this gap. When Democrats matched GOP turnout rates (as in 2008 and 2018), they performed exceptionally well. When the gap widened (as in 2010, 2014, and 2024), they struggled. Moreover, our own research finds that progressive candidates are slightly more effective at mobilizing their base and increasing turnout among registered Democrats. This finding comes from tracking the voting behavior of over 120 million individuals across five election cycles, a design that isolates the effect of candidate ideology by comparing the same voters across different elections.

Second, local politics has been swamped by national tides. In our hyperpolarized system, voters increasingly choose Team Blue or Team Red based on national sentiment, not the ideology of their local candidate. Every Democrat—from the progressive Alexandria Ocasio-Cortez to the moderate Jared Golden—now rises or falls with the party brand. When inflation hit 8 percent, voters didn't parse ideological differences; they punished the party in power. When Donald Trump was unpopular in 2018, Democrats of all stripes saw sizable gains.

This reality is well-documented in political science. One of us—Grumbach—has written a whole book showing how voters have become more attentive to national news and how state parties have increasingly become agents of their national counterparts. The result is that congressional elections now function more like national referendums, where a candidate's individual positioning is often overwhelmed by these larger forces. To be sure, candidate quality still matters some, but it matters less, and moderation itself does not seem to be an especially important quality.

Third, being moderate doesn't necessarily mean having a more popular platform. As political scientist David Broockman has shown, voters who appear moderate often hold a mix of extreme positions rather than consistently centrist ones: confiscate billionaire wealth but also ban abortion. There is no coherent "center" to triangulate toward, and a candidate who tries may end up pleasing no one.

Fourth, the median voter theorem may underestimate the role of political leadership in the current environment. The Trump era is full of examples of voters seeking a leader who "tells it like it is." These voters want authenticity and disruption, not careful ideological positioning. An appeal to moderation may completely miss the mark with voters who want a candidate who projects strength and a willingness to challenge the system.

This desire for authenticity is closely related to the idea that voters "follow the leader": politicians influence voters' policy attitudes, not the other way around. Michael Barber and Jeremy C. Pope have a creative analysis of this phenomenon focused on Donald Trump's contradictory policy statements. (Evidence for this theory appears in Gabriel Lenz's

2012 book, *Follow the Leader*, as well as in much of the work of Achen and Bartels.) Trump has garnered the support of the most anti-vaccine voters in the United States, despite having overseen the creation of Operation Warp Speed in 2020 to rapidly develop COVID-19 vaccines. And he has taken flatly contradictory positions on abortion and the minimum wage, sometimes in the same interview. When researchers show voters one of these statements, many adopt that position. The leader shapes the followers, not the other way around.

The median voter theorem made sense in an era of stable coalitions, low polarization, and localized elections. That era is over.

But this dynamic has an important precondition: voters must already identify with the leader. Trump can shift positions freely because his supporters are following him, not his platform. The policy positions are downstream of the relationship. For candidates still trying to build that relationship, the calculus is different. Strategic repositioning can signal inauthenticity, which is precisely what prevents the bond from forming in the first place.

The recent history of high-profile Democratic moderates confirms this. Consider Jared Golden, who since 2019 has represented Maine's 2nd congressional district, one of the few districts in the country that has split its ticket for Trump and a Democratic House member. Golden is the archetypal moderate: a Marine veteran who broke with his party on key votes, opposed Nancy Pelosi for House Speaker, and carefully cultivated an independent brand. If the moderation thesis were correct, Golden should have been thriving. Instead, by October 2025 his favorability had collapsed to 16 percent, and 57 percent of his constituents said he did not deserve reelection. He chose not to run again this year. And he is not alone. Kyrsten Sinema, the most prominent Senate moderate of the Trump era, offers perhaps the starkest warning. By late 2022, her strategy of triangulation had achieved a rare feat: she was unpopular with Democrats, Republicans, and independents alike. Having alienated her base without securing the opposition, she, too, declined to seek reelection.

Finally, strategic moderation often undermines the very credibility it seeks to build. When candidates without the leadership clout of people like Trump or Manchin shift positions to chase the political center, voters see them as unprincipled, not pragmatic. The strategic calculation is often transparent, validating an opponent's charge that the candidate lacks core beliefs. When center-left parties in Europe adopt anti-immigration positions to counter the far right, it brings them no electoral benefit; if anything, researchers have found, strategies that "accommodate" right-wing positions "lead to more voters defecting to the radical right." Democrats who chase moderate Republicans by adopting their frames risk the same outcome.

The median voter theorem made sense in an era of stable coalitions, low polarization, and localized elections. That era is over. Democrats need strategies built for this new reality.

IF MODERATION ISN'T SURE to deliver victory, and if popularism leads to paralysis, what should Democrats do? The honest answer is that nobody knows for certain. Our issue with popularism is its air of certainty. There is reasonable room for debate about the virtues of particular kinds of moderation in particular contexts. But political elites should not interpret the results of biased statistical analyses as a form of scientific justification for any political strategy, something we see frequently in recent discourse.

The reality is that electoral politics has entered an era of profound volatility, when yesterday's certainties become today's mistakes. We are not making a general case for running to the left instead of to the center but for dispensing with outdated conventional wisdom.

Instead, we favor experimentation and exploration. Embracing these requires expanding our sense of possibility and the range of our explorations, partly by paying close attention to what has worked in other countries that have faced democratic backsliding. Taking inspiration from their experiences, we draw three important lessons.

Reframe the Battlefield

The most effective opposition in a polarized society doesn't try to win a few converts on an entrenched battlefield; it redraws the map

entirely. Successful anti-authoritarian movements do not win by soft-
ening their positions. They win by building unlikely coalitions around a
broadly resonant grievance.

One promising possibility is to focus on corruption. Anti-corruption
has been a powerful axis of political mobilization throughout history
and across democracies. It is not a poll-tested "issue" like health care or
immigration; it is a frame that reorganizes politics around a fundamental
question of legitimacy. And the conditions for such a frame are present.
A May 2025 poll from Yale and George Mason found more Americans said
they are "very worried" about government corruption than about the cost
of living or the economy. This frustration is rooted in a deep-seated belief
that the system is rigged; a recent YouGov survey, for instance, found
that a staggering 73 percent of Americans believe a member of Congress
would be likely to accept a bribe if offered one. The revelations about
Clarence Thomas accepting undisclosed gifts from billionaire donors, or
members of Congress trading stocks on nonpublic information, confirm
what many already suspect: the rules don't apply to the powerful.

The choice now is to transform the party's strategy to meet the scale of the threat, or to risk the end of democratic self-governance itself.

The energy generated by disclosure of the Epstein files points in the
same direction: large numbers of people saw a club of powerful insiders
acting with impunity. Focusing on corruption shifts the debate from di-
visive ideological questions to a simple moral choice: Are you on the side
of the people, or of a rigged system?

Build Anti-Establishment Credibility

An anti-corruption platform is useless without anti-establishment
credibility, which many Democratic leaders now lack. They need to position themselves as the party that will take on the real elites—billionaires
buying Supreme Court justices, corporations price-gouging families,
insiders trading stocks on classified briefings.

This will require genuine, costly reform—and self-criticism—that
goes beyond rhetoric: ending deceptive fundraising practices, rejecting

corporate PAC money, and championing popular measures like banning congressional stock trading. Recruiting authentic, working-class candidates—nurses, teachers, veterans—is also crucial, not as a matter of ideological positioning, but as a demonstration that the party is not beholden to the same professional class. Let a thousand flowers bloom; these candidates should put forward platforms and campaigns based on what they authentically think would help the country, not what might attract donors, please crypto lobbyists, or satisfy a popularist's survey samples. Action, not messaging, is the only path to earning the credibility needed to lead this fight.

Boost Turnout

Most critically, Democrats must fix their turnout crisis.

While much of the punditry has focused on swings toward Trump among young men and Latinos in 2024, the turnout gap between registered Democrats and Republicans was much more devastating. This turnout gap appeared across all voter categories—among reliable voters from 2020, sporadic voters who voted in 2020 but sat out in 2024, and newly registered voters. The gap between Black and white Americans reached 10.9 percentage points—the widest in over three decades, as Black participation dropped more sharply than white. Youth turnout was also down from 2020. The Republican turnout advantage in 2024 exceeded both 2020 and 2016. It's true that nonvoters likely leaned slightly toward Trump over Harris in November 2024, but large segments of these nonvoters were progressive young people and most others might have been persuaded by a more credible Democratic Party.

The popularist strategy pours resources into chasing a dwindling number of swing voters while neglecting the millions of disengaged citizens who power its victories. A policy-based appeal that proposes incremental changes to a status quo that many see as fundamentally unfair and corrupt is not enough to overcome the deep-seated cynicism that keeps many voters home. More promising is to mobilize people who believe the system is rigged with a credible promise to un-rig it. A genuine anti-corruption fight provides the moral clarity and purpose needed to energize the base, young voters, and even disillusioned conservatives disgusted by a system they believe has been captured by special interests. It answers the fundamental strategic question not of how to appeal to the median voter, but of how to create a new, mobilized electorate by giving them a cause larger than any single candidate.

The false choice between "moderate" and "progressive" has trapped Democrats in an irrelevant debate while democracy hangs in the balance. The real divide isn't left versus center—it's whether Democrats view Trump as an aberration to be waited out or as an authoritarian threat that requires an extraordinary response. Journalist Ronald Brownstein recently identified this fault line: those who view authoritarianism as a "distraction" from kitchen-table issues versus those who see it as the existential crisis defining all other questions. The "distraction" camp still operates by 1990s rules, counseling moderation and patience, trusting failed institutions.

This brings us back to a crucial point: successful anti-authoritarian movements don't win by moderating their positions on a traditional left-right axis but by creating an entirely new one. They mobilize previously disengaged citizens by framing the struggle not as a contest over policy, but as a fight for the fundamental fairness of the system itself.

DEMOCRATS CAN KEEP DEBATING whether to stand five degrees or fifteen degrees left of center, fine-tuning messages drowned out by the latest Trump spectacle. They can chase moderate voters our data shows won't materialize while their base stays home. They can maintain faith that reasonableness will eventually triumph.

Or they can accept the evidence: the old rules are dead. In a nationalized media environment with an authoritarian movement capturing one major party, electoral politics has become existential conflict. This requires not moderation but mobilization, not positioning but purpose, not just messaging but genuine reform to prove that Democrats will fight for democracy itself by first attacking the corruption that rots it from within.

Scholars of democratic breakdown know that moments like this demand institutional coordination, civil society mobilization, and the political courage to name and confront the authoritarian threat on its weakest flank. Every democracy facing this challenge has learned you don't defeat authoritarians by being more reasonable. You defeat them by being more determined and by uniting the country against their most visible vulnerability: their corruption.

History won't judge Democrats on whether they were moderate enough. It will judge them on whether they fought hard enough, and smart enough, when democracy was threatened. The politics of careful positioning and poll-tested moderation have been tested, and on their own, they have failed to deliver the victories needed to protect democracy. The choice now is to transform the party's strategy to meet the scale of the threat, or to fail. In this contest, failure is not just an electoral defeat; it may be the end of democratic self-governance. **BR**

SOCIALISM IN ONE CITY

David Austin Walsh

Z OHRAN MAMDANI IS NOW the mayor of New York City. Amid the chaos unleashed by Trump in the first weeks of 2026, it can be easy to lose sight of the truly seismic shift in politics his mayoralty represents.

To recap: an obscure, thirty-four-year-old state assemblyman and member of the Democratic Socialists of America, who a year ago could barely fill a seminar room at New York University, beat both incumbent mayor Eric Adams and former governor Andrew Cuomo by running on an unapologetically progressive ticket, critical of ICE and Israel as much as rents being too damn high. India Walton came close to a similar upset in Buffalo four years ago, but this time the socialists prevailed. In his inaugural address on New Year's Day, sworn in by Bernie Sanders and quoting Fiorello La Guardia, Mamdani spoke of building a city "'far greater and more beautiful' for the hungry and the poor." Handing out free tickets to a theater festival in January, he spoke of his vision of a city "where we make it possible for working people to afford lives of joy, of art, of rest, of expression." When's the last time you heard a politician talk like this?

To the establishment it sounds like so much juvenile poetry. Real governing, the self-styled adults in the room insist, happens in prose. Many of them aren't just predicting a rude awakening; they are actively seeking to tank Mamdani's time in office. But the forces of reaction are right about one thing: the stakes are very high. The U.S. left needs Mamdani's mayorship to be successful—not because it will resolve intraleft fights over electoralism once and for all but because, in the eyes of a watchful public, it will determine whether social democracy can become politically legitimate in the United States.

The ultimate test is governance. On this point, the Mamdani administration and the more mainstream "abundance" liberals of the Democratic Party are agreed: a viable left-liberal politics needs to be able to point to a track record of success. Chicago mayor Brandon Johnson offers a cautionary tale. Like Mamdani, Johnson won a hard-fought campaign in 2023 against an incumbent mayor and a Republican-backed protest candidate. And like Mamdani's victory, his was made possible through mass grassroots mobilization of supporters and progressive allies. But Johnson's popularity plummeted almost immediately after his election, dragged down by perceptions of cronyism and incompetence, and while his poll numbers have recovered somewhat since the depths of 2024, he is still almost twenty points underwater.

Implementing a truly transformative agenda in the country's largest city—which also just happens to be the center of global finance—could reset the narrative. The "public good" and the "commons," alien phrases in the kleptocratic hellscape of neoliberal America, might prove closer in reach than ever before.

TROTSKY FAMOUSLY REJECTED the possibility of socialism in one country. What about in one city? Successful social democratic politics at the municipal level really can work, but it requires rethinking decades of received wisdom about political economy.

The starting point is reconsidering elite-driven growth as the lodestone of urban planning and development. As historian Daniel Wortel-London chronicles in his recent book *The Menace of Prosperity*, urban policymakers assumed for much of the twentieth century that economic development is directly downstream of "enticing and retaining the wealthy."

This was not always the case. New York City used to be dominated by real estate, services, and then light manufacturing. The latter industry fueled social mobility after it was organized, making the International Ladies Garment Workers Union one of the most influential unions in the country in the 1920s and 1930s. But this model of political economy, grounded in the high wages of union labor, began to collapse by mid-century as suburbanization, white flight, and the decline of domestic manufacturing hollowed out the tax base of American cities.

One response was to attract and consolidate businesses in urban cores. Chicago achieved some success with this approach under

Richard J. Daley in the 1960s and 1970s, with Sears Tower a lasting testament. Another was revenue sharing—basically, pooling the growing suburban tax base into a metropolitan area-wide fund. Minneapolis and St. Paul took this approach in the 1970s, creating a Metropolitan Council backed by the state government.

The sneering haters of all political stripes are right about one thing: the stakes of Mamdani's mayorship are very high.

But each approach had limits. Corporate offices in the Chicago Loop didn't reverse population decline, nor did they dismantle the prevailing racial order. In 1966 Martin Luther King Jr. went head to head with Daley's liberal machine, speaking before an audience in the tens of thousands gathered in Soldier Field: "Let us be dissatisfied until every socially oppressive ghetto and rat-infested slum is plunged into the junk heaps of our nation and Negroes and whites live side by side in decent, safe, and sanitary housing." The Twin Cities, for their part, were utterly dependent on a supportive state government and urban cores that were still overwhelmingly white. Facing its own massive financial crisis in the 1970s, New York City opted for a hybrid approach. Like Chicago, it would try to keep as many corporate offices as possible within city limits, but it would also court the mega-rich to inflate the tax base and attract the service industries that cater to them.

The result has been a deeply inequitable city, one leading the national affordability crisis. Wortel-London is refreshingly blunt: rampant inequality, in and of itself, carries a massive social cost. It distorts the body politic and reorients society around servicing wealth. It distorts politics too, because it makes catering to the wealthy the guiding principle of municipal governance. A city comprised primarily of extraordinarily wealthy people and their professional-class courtiers means more taxable income but also fewer people making claims on social services—which, among other things, can mean a tax reduction. As the problematic poor get pushed out, the city effectively becomes another gated community. Dylan Gottlieb's forthcoming history of the yuppies—that Reagan-era neologism for young urban professionals — makes clear they weren't simply the shock troops of gentrification; they were policymakers' pawns, recruited to achieve just this.

Ironically, the project seems to have worked *too* well. Mamdani haters sneer that he owes the election to the so-called "Commie Corridor," a strip of neighborhoods running from Astoria in Queens to Prospect Park in Brooklyn and consisting primarily of well-educated professionals fretting about their downward mobility. The observation is meant to delegitimize — look at these entitled rich kids cosplaying at communism! — but support for the old paradigm really has collapsed. The yuppies, at least in New York, are now the socialists, and reform is the watchword of the day. Will threats of capital flight from hedge fund manager Bill Ackman and his billionaire friends get in the way?

MAMDANI IS HARDLY the first socialist mayor to navigate these challenges. He's not even the first DSA member to become mayor of New York — that was David Dinkins, elected in 1989, though with much less reliance on the organization than Mamdani.

But it's another mayoralty that may hold the clearest lessons for today. Before beginning his long and steady march to technocratic Cold War liberalism, Walter Lippmann was a card-carrying member of the Socialist Party of America and served as a deputy to fellow Socialist George Lunn, who was elected mayor of Schenectady, New York, in 1911. Lippmann only lasted a few months in the role, disillusioned by what he felt were Lunn's compromises and political opportunism. But the experience prompted reflections worth revisiting now.

In a letter to another Socialist comrade, Carl D. Thompson, two years later, Lippmann harshly criticized Lunn but also noted the bind he faced. "Where is the allegiance of Socialists elected by non-Socialists?" he asked. Lunn refused to raise taxes to pay for municipal services out of fear it would "alienate the property-holders whose votes decided the election." But "it is quite clearly the business of a Socialist administration," Lippmann wrote, "to cut into the returns of property, take as much of them as possible to be spent for social purposes." This is precisely the vision that Wortel-London lays out: economic development and growth as *social* goods, not ends in themselves.

The ends—and the broader vision of society underpinning them—really do matter. "Take the municipal ownership and operation of subways," Lippmann went on. Both progressive reformers and socialists across the country supported public ownership of mass transit systems, at the time owned and operated by private companies. But the goals were different. "The profits on a socialistically conducted subway would be a direct transfer from private dividends to the people," Lippmann explained. "The profits on a reformist subway would be a transfer from stockholders to taxpayers."

Will threats of capital flight from hedge fund manager Bill Ackman and his billionaire friends get in the way?

In other words, there is a big difference between a public good administered *as* a public good and one that exists primarily for the benefit of the middle classes. The distinction also implies a difference in messaging and moral leadership, as many contemporary writers have observed. Even the *New York Times*'s David Leonhardt, hardly a Sanders-Mamdani partisan, has stressed the "perils of invisible government," criticizing Obama and Biden for aspiring to do public good as quietly as possible. Routing policy through Cass Sunstein–style "nudges," or what political scientist Suzanne Mettler has deemed the "submerged state," is a recipe for political disaster. The whole point of socialist politics is to make state power and state capacity *explicit* in a way that liberals have long eschewed.

Lippmann concluded his letter on an ambiguous note, at once rejecting electoralism—he believed Lunn's compromises dashed any chance of genuine socialist power—while affirming the importance of governance in building socialist credibility. For Lippmann, socialists needed practical political and administrative experience, in part to overcome their reputation, deserved or not, for political incompetence. "I have watched a local of two hundred Socialists trying to audit fifty-cent bills by majority vote," he lamented. The solution, he thought, was to build experience and credibility through unions and cooperatives.

Unfortunately, in the twenty-first century, that is simply not a viable alternative. One result of the decline of these traditional training grounds for socialist governance, as Ned Resnikoff recently pointed out in *Dissent*, is that too much of the left remains in thrall to what could be called David Graeberism: an anarchist, anti-system outlook that flourished with Occupy Wall Street, resolutely hostile to working within the state. Mamdani and his political allies, above all Alexandria Ocasio-Cortez, represent a very different tradition, invested in using bureaucracy to achieve democratic socialist ends. For better or worse, now that Mamdani is the most powerful socialist in the country, they have to show they have the chops to actually govern.

SO FAR, AT LEAST, things are looking good.

The specter of capital flight hasn't materialized. And in policy terms, Mamdani spent his first weeks issuing a blitz of executive orders making good on campaign promises. He revived the Mayor's Office to Protect Tenants and installed tenant organizer Cea Weaver to lead it. He brought former Federal Trade Commission chair Lina Khan aboard as his affordability czar. In a genuinely shocking moment, at least for those who remember the infamously terrible relationship between Mayor Bill de Blasio and Governor Andrew Cuomo, Mamdani and Governor Kathy Hochul jointly announced a plan for universal child care for all New Yorkers between the ages of two and four. Legislation was introduced in December to advance Mamdani's vision of a new Department of Community Safety that would work to "prevent violence before it happens by taking a public health approach to safety." And perhaps most significantly, his Executive Order 7 set up an Office of Mass Engagement, superseding an older civic engagement program, to promote democratic governance.

Critics on the left say these are hardly revolutionary transformations. They are right, but they could stand to recall Lippmann's point about ends. These are good, solid initiatives that liberals and progressives—and even erstwhile centrists like Hochul—can get behind. Even more important, they are being deployed to achieve democratic socialist political goals, without sacrificing an internationalist vision to boot. There certainly are limits to what the Mamdani administration can accomplish. New York has a strong mayor system, but he faces a relatively conservative city council, and while Hochul is certainly a more reliable partner than Cuomo, Albany always looms ominously in the background. But the mayor *does* have considerable authority he can exercise through executive orders and staffing decisions, and Mamdani has been aggressive in using it thus far.

Of course, using power effectively requires weathering scurrilous political attacks. Ironically, on this score, the over-the-top anticommunist and Islamophobic fearmongering about Mamdani seems to have functioned as a kind of battle testing. Who can forget the gutter racist AI-generated ads the Cuomo campaign tweeted claiming that Mamdani would release violent criminals back onto the streets, legalize sex trafficking, and globalize the intifada? Bari Weiss's *The Free Press* has run at least half a dozen articles since the election about Mamdani's alleged antisemitism, one depicting him as a Third Worldist working to bring the Algerian revolution to our shores. Liberal blogger Noah Smith intimated that Mamdani represents "the growth of Islamoleftism in America." The smear campaign seems to go beyond time-honored reflex; it looks more like they understand Mamdani's generational talent — on par with AOC as Sanders's successor — and are desperate to contain it. But the old slanders aren't working, and the insecurity is driving them mad.

There's a big difference between a public good administered as a public good and one that exists primarily for the benefit of the middle classes.

At bottom, the reason for these ridiculous and racist slurs is the same as the reason for the relentless conspiracizing about Barack Obama. Like Obama, Mamdani is a very popular, charming, and telegenic politician with an "exotic" name and brown skin. Unlike Obama, Mamdani actually *is* a Muslim and isn't beholden to compromise and consensus. The fact that he isn't afraid of conflict — isn't, as Obama described himself in his post-presidential memoir, "conservative in temperament" — makes his success even more dangerous to the center-right mainstream. Yet even Trump, who for years demanded that Obama release his birth certificate, clearly relished being in the new mayor's presence at their Oval Office meeting in November. Most of all Mamdani has charisma, and Trump knows better than most just how far you can go with it. An important segment of Mamdani's electoral coalition was South Asian voters in the outer boroughs who broke for Trump in 2024.

All this seems to have helped Mamdani not cave to anxieties over optics. He has successfully resisted bad-faith attacks from the *Times* and allies of Eric Adams over failing to appoint a Black deputy mayor, a transparent ploy by the Democratic establishment to deploy identity politics against Mamdani and perpetuate a form of ethnic patronage politics that should have long been left in the dust. Mamdani has also refused to throw the Palestinian solidarity movement under the bus despite endless goading by the Democratic establishment. As his recent condemnation of a pro-Hamas demonstration in front of a Queens synagogue demonstrates, his approach has been pragmatic and strategic.

And to return to the urban development front, the new mayor has also stood by Weaver, his housing appointee, after the *New York Post* reported on tweets she made during the 2010s supposedly demonstrating her hatred of white people. (Weaver herself is white.) Vaguely tongue-in-cheek posting during Peak Woke, the administration seems to recognize, should not lead to political self-immolation in 2026. Weaver is a well-respected policy expert who has a stellar track record in policy and organizing circles. Writing for *Phenomenal World* last October, she concluded that a rent freeze—a plank of Mamdani's platform—was essentially inevitable given that New Yorkers simply cannot afford more rent increases but that it needed to be paired with code enforcement, and more importantly public investment, where the City of New York acts as a "quasi-community land trust." In essence, Weaver wants to use the power of the state to suppress the rampant real estate speculation that is undermining affordability in New York City, and invest that money in public housing.

This, too, would warm the young Lippmann's socialist heart. The point is not to freeze rents simply to deliver to constituents—although that is certainly an added benefit—but to begin to reimagine an urban political economy not based around the principle of constantly inflating real estate prices for the benefit of investors and property owners. One of Weaver's tweets cited by the *Post* says that "private property including

and kind of ESPECIALLY homeownership is a weapon of white supremacy masquerading as 'wealth building' public policy." That may not be
winning campaign language (as Weaver no doubt understands), especially as the movement tries to grow and build power in white-majority
districts it will need to take back Congress. But there is a fundamental
truth to the analysis that isn't rebutted by the fact that some people of
color own their homes in New York's outer boroughs.

For decades policymakers have assumed that rising property values are an unquestioned good for development and tax purposes and
should be the goal of urban public policy, and thanks to a staggering (and
growing) racial wealth gap, any institution that facilitates the reproduc-
tion of this model—including the prevailing system of homeownership
and home loans and everything tied to it—really does perpetuate white
supremacy. It would do so even in the absence of redlining and racist
real estate agents, but these things are very real too and only compound
the problem.

Weaver and Mamdani are rightly challenging this paradigm, not
out of vengeful malice—which is how every dominant class experiences
any egalitarian movement anyway—but in the name and spirit of genuine universalism. This shift in political imagination is long overdue,
and the power it has won shows just how much the U.S. left has matured
politically. In the past ten years we've gone from tweets and articles in
little magazines decrying racial capitalism to developing a thoughtful
and granular theory of politics that can win despite the decades-long
collapse of labor and that seeks to use the power of the state for the
public good, mobilized by a multiethnic coalition of downwardly mobile
professionals and working-class people. If it works, we have a model for
the nation. **BR**

THE WAR NO ONE WANTED

Photographs by Salih Basheer
Text by Joshua Craze

November 11, 2025, New York City

D**EAR SALIH,**
You asked me to write an essay to accompany your book, *The Return*, and gave me one rule. "Don't discuss the photographs." You told me: "I want people to see the images on their own terms." This essay is written in counterpoint.

I arrived in New York three weeks ago, after a long trip to South Sudan's flooded conflict zones. Walking through the city, en route to dinner, I reflected on the fact that all my Sudanese friends are posing the same questions: Is anywhere safe? Is a return possible? Some inquire from Tawila, having fled the massacre in El Fasher. Others ask from bedrooms in Nairobi, shelters in New York, or the camp in Kiryandongo, Uganda.

I was to eat with a friend whose family is from Gezira State, in the center of Sudan. In January 2025, Wad Medani, the state capital, had been recaptured by the Sudanese army. Videos of the massacres that had occurred, taken by the perpetrators, were one of the few sources of information we had about the assault. Not for the first time, I thought how unjust it is that history is literally being recorded by the victors, and that in the absence of another record we are forced to confront these documents of savagery.

My friend and I ate pilau for dinner, surrounded by people from all over the world who had come to New York for sanctuary or work, for pleasure or duty. My friend was disconsolate. "It's over," she said. "Even if there was a ceasefire, even if there was peace, to what would we be returning? The Khartoum I know no longer exists. You cannot build a life from ruins. There is no going back." I was reminded of a line in a poem by the Palestinian writer Mahmoud Darwish: "We travel like other people, but we return to nowhere."

Perhaps it's not helpful for the expert to hold up his hands and announce his confusion, but I think there is a clue here, something that might help us comprehend the war's enormous complexity.

Writing in November 2025, after the devastations of El Fasher, it is hard to recall the uncertainties of the war's early days, back in April 2023, when I dared hope it might end quickly. Friends resolved to stay in Khartoum, even as the Sudanese army and the Rapid Support Forces (RSF) fought for control of its streets, reducing family homes and favored coffee spots to rubble. One friend fretted about her birds. "I would leave," she told me plaintively, "but who will take care of them?" In the end, she went, joining the flows of people searching for a way out of the war. Some fled to Egypt, enduring or expiring in long sunburned queues at the border. Others went to Jeddah or even to Abu Dhabi—the capital of the United Arab Emirates (UAE), the major sponsor of the militia razing Sudan. Many friends came south to the Joda border crossing. The lucky ones who still had dollars in their pockets went to Juba, South Sudan's capital, and then made their way to Uganda. Those without means were driven to Maban county, where in August 2023, I saw the UN refugee agency pile doctors and teachers onto trucks, drive them into the bush, beyond the reach of any phone network, and curtly inform them that *here* is where they would make their new lives.

Can there be life without a return? A few months after the war began I was in Nairobi, smoking shisha with a Sudanese friend, freshly arrived from Khartoum. We talked about how different the tobacco in Nairobi tasted, and how Kenyans, inexplicably, never make time to drink tea. He said: "I have just one question: Do I need to buy a mattress?" He meant: How long will I need to stay here? How much of a life do I need to imagine? I told him that he will, unfortunately, need to buy a bed and more besides. His mouth hardened. Then we talked of Khartoum, as it was before the war, and we discussed the brave women and men of the Emergency Response Rooms, as they are now, all over Sudan, providing food and health services to the needy, despite being persecuted by both the army and the RSF. As we talked of Sudans old and new, he smiled, and I thought, if I were a photographer, I would have liked to take his picture.

I AM SUPPOSED TO be an expert. I write reports about the war. Diplomats with concerned brows ask me for my opinion on where the conflict is going. Will the RSF take Babanusa? Will its drones strike Khartoum again? Are the UAE interested in peace? The answer to the last question seems obvious to me—it's contained in images of the bright new weapons the Emirates have festooned on the RSF, with as much largesse as Sheikh Mansour bin Zayed al-Nahyan uses to outfit the Manchester City front-line. I try to answer the other questions the diplomats pose, but under my peacocked expertise, I'm confused. This war, I cannot understand it all. Perhaps it's not helpful for the expert to hold up his hands and announce his confusion, but I think there is a clue here, something that might help us comprehend the war's enormous complexity. My confusion has its roots in a demonstration I attended in Khartoum, back in October 2021.

The stage should first be set. Omar al-Bashir was an army brigadier who came to power in a coup d'état in 1989, with the backing of Hassan al-Turabi and the National Islamic Front. He took over a state gripped by a civil war fought against a rebel group in the south of the country. Sudan was also struggling with a deep economic crisis, partly brought about by the punishing austerity politics promoted by the country's debtors in the Global North. From this unpromising material, Bashir forged an enduring

form of rule, one we are still living with today. The state abandoned the peripheries of the country, and rather than fight its civil war using the Sudanese army, it outsourced its monopoly of violence to militias, who waged a counterinsurgency on the cheap, taking loot in lieu of wages. To control the militias, Bashir privatized the state, turning it into a multitude of rivalrous fiefdoms, ruled over by his security services, each of which built up its own economic empire. The Sudanese army took control of banking and construction. To the riparian cities along the Nile, Bashir offered a Faustian pact: accept cheap commodities and subsidies for fuel and wheat, but know that their import requires foreign currency, obtained from the sale of resources produced in the peripheries, which would have to be pacified.

The war in southern Sudan finally ended in 2005, after twenty-two long years, with a promise that the rebels would have a regional government and the chance to hold a referendum on independence in 2011. By then, another war had begun, one that has never really ended. In 2003, a rebellion started in Darfur in protest at political marginalization and land grabs by nomadic Arab herders backed by the government. Bashir decided to repeat the playbook he deployed in the south of Sudan, and outsourced the conflict to local militias. He armed Arab nomads, which were nicknamed the Janjaweed. They laid waste to Darfur. Their modus operandi was to burn villages, kill civilians, and help themselves to the land of the displaced. Among their number was a young commander, Muhammad Hamdan Dagalo, nicknamed Hemedti. His raids across North Darfur in 2006 were particularly brutal: he raped women and tortured men. As much as they were fighting for Bashir's regime, the Janjaweed were also pursuing more local goals: consolidating territorial control, and forcing non-Arab groups into camps for the internally displaced. It is these camps that have been razed over the past two years: the refuges of one war have become the charnel houses of the next.

Back in the early 2000s, Bashir's counterinsurgency on the cheap proved expensive. Militia leaders, promised ranks and payments, soon became disaffected with Khartoum. They would fight against each other, and also against the government. Fearing a coup d'état, Bashir created the RSF, which he conceived of as both a counterinsurgency force and a Praetorian guard, designed to coup-proof his regime. Hemedti soon rose to lead the militia. While the state paid and trained his fighters, Hemedti expanded the RSF's business interests, taking over gold mines in Darfur, and dispatching his troops to Yemen to fight as mercenaries for the UAE and Saudi Arabia. The Sudanese army got in on the act, too, and also sent men to Yemen. That force's leader was an army general by the name of Abdel Fattah al-Burhan.

Back in Sudan, Bashir's regime was under pressure. In 2011, South Sudan voted to secede, and Khartoum lost 75 percent of its oil revenue. Facing economic crisis, Bashir desperately tried to diversify Sudan's income streams by getting into gold mining, just as a gold rush was sweeping the Sahel and global prices surged. It didn't work. The state failed to control the production of artisanal gold, which is largely smuggled out of Sudan. The boom in gold mining instead enabled Hemedti to entrench his dominion in Darfur by running mining sites and displacing other militia forces. Few in Khartoum were happy with Hemedti's success. He was an interloper from the peripheries, a barely educated camel rustler with pretensions to power. In Darfur, the Arab militias lorded it over non-Arab groups, even if the distinctions between them were historically very mutable and became definitive only through the devastations of war. In Khartoum, the Arabs of Darfur were foreigners, "Chadians" —uneducated savages not fit to run the country.

Little came of Bashir's effort to save his regime. By 2018, the economy was flailing. The government cut subsidies to wheat and fuel, breaking its pact with Sudan's cities. Protests began in the peripheries, but soon spread. I remember delightedly watching the demonstrations. The resistance committees that led the protests were a photographic negative of Bashir's neighborhood committees, which kept a close eye on political activities and produced an atmosphere of paranoia and mistrust. Where the regime was repressive, the resistance committees were joyful. While Bashir had withdrawn services from Sudan's poor and concentrated power in the hands of the security organs, the resistance committees had offered free health care and mutual aid, and were explicitly nonviolent. At protests, people would chant *kol al-balad Darfur*: the whole country is Darfur. For a moment, it felt like the racism and violence of Bashir's predatory state would be undone and a new social contract forged.

The protests intensified in 2019, and the regime met them with violence. The security services became uneasy. It was one thing to kill people in the peripheries and quite another to mow down the youth of Khartoum, many of whom came from the families of soldiers and politicians. One day in April, Bashir allegedly gave an order to open fire on the protesters. By the next day, he was gone. The military controlled the state. What a beautiful moment that was! The heavy certainty of the dictatorship dissolved into the air. Slogans celebrating the army were graffitied onto Khartoum's walls. But the goals of the protesters and those of the army were not consonant. The security services hoped that by deposing Bashir, they could conserve their economic empires. The protesters, in contrast, wanted a civilian government, not a new military dictator.

The Sudanese army and the RSF found common cause in repressing the demonstrations. On June 3, the security services violently invaded a sit-in outside the military headquarters, leaving more than 120 protesters dead and some nine hundred injured. Despite the violence, the demonstrations continued. On June 30, the thirtieth anniversary of Bashir's coup, hundreds of thousands of people marched against the junta. I recently spoke to a friend, now exiled in Cairo. He said:

"I became a human being during those protests. I found out I had power. That I did not have to be afraid. I felt like I was growing in size, literally. They will never take that from me."

What happened after the march will be debated for a century to come. Civilian politicians from Sudan's established parties opened up negotiations with the military. International actors, including the United States, Britain, Saudi Arabia, and the UAE, pressured the army to enter a transitional government with the politicians. Many of my friends think protests should have continued and a general strike called. It was a moment, they hold, in which the military could have been pushed out of power. Others disagree: more bloodshed had to be avoided, they say. Ultimately, a compromise was reached: a transitional government was created in August 2019, with a sovereign council composed of military officers and civilian politicians, prior to elections promised for 2022. Burhan would serve as the council's head and Hemedti as his deputy. Abdalla Hamdok, a UN economist, was to be prime minister and the head of a technocratic cabinet.

Viewed from the street, Hamdok's time in government seemed like a sellout. His economic policies abandoned the progressive socioeconomic agenda propounded by the protesters in favor of economic austerity and the elimination of subsidies, measures designed to win the sympathies of the International Monetary Fund and the World Bank. Relations with Israel were normalized (as if they could ever be normal), and in response, Trump promised to remove sanctions. Little was done to break up the military's economic empire. Some of my friends served with Hamdok's cabinet, and they didn't think he was simply selling out. "We needed allies," they explained to me. "Without the international community, we could never have fought against the old regime," one friend whispered, in a quiet garden in a residential area of Khartoum, away from prying ears.

It was the people versus the military, and the junta was losing. The only thing that could save it would be a war.

By 2021, two years into the transitional government, discontent with Hamdok was rising, but so were popular fears of a coup. I visited Khartoum that fall, attending a demonstration on October 21. I remember gathering—as is traditional—before a burning tire in Burri, listening to speeches and conversations twirl around the thick black smoke. Anxious European diplomats were texting me: "But do they favor Hamdok?" I wanted to laugh. The protesters' opinions on Hamdok differed, but that was not the focus of the demonstration. The people wanted an end to military rule. Behind that simple, powerful demand, there was a feeling, experienced by everyone marching that day. Thousands of people had organized together. Proud young women and men went in front, scouting out the positions of the security services. Groups of older people sang revolutionary songs just behind them. *But what are they saying?* the diplomats asked, holed up in their embassies. I replied by holding up my phone to the din of the crowd.

That night, I put my head down on the pillow and couldn't sleep. I didn't think about the intelligence operatives who had taken up residence in the lobby of my cheap hotel. Nor about the rumors of a coup. I thought: Is there a soul in Sudan tonight that wants the RSF or the Sudanese army to be in power? I knew they were out there, those sad souls, but such was the power of the protests that I couldn't imagine them.

I left Khartoum for Addis Ababa three days later. The next morning, Burhan and Hemedti launched their coup d'état, pushing the civilians out of power. Anxious media commentators talked of a season of coups, placing

Sudan next to Guinea and Mali, but I knew that it was not the same. The idea that Burhan could be Abdel Fattah el-Sisi, ruling Sudan with an iron hand, was risible. Both the RSF and the Sudanese army lacked any real social base. Neither group had the religious support that allowed Bashir to rule during the 1990s. While the RSF was backed by the Arab groups that had profited from the devastation of Darfur, such support stopped at the region's borders—Hemedti's efforts to build up the militia as a multi-ethnic force had been unsuccessful. The Sudanese army faced widespread unpopularity due to its role in repressing the revolution.

Here is my confusion. This is a war that no one wanted. Everybody hoped the military would leave power. They may have taken control in a coup, but I knew they were weak.

So it proved. I next visited Khartoum a year later. The city looked scruffier than I had ever seen it, with trash piling up and walls falling down. The junta was not exactly flourishing. Burhan and Hemedti had cast about for a civilian face for their regime. Hamdok had been brought back, a month after the coup occurred, only to resign six weeks later after massive protests. In cafés and at music events, I found my friends still discussing politics, still singing, and still organizing against the generals. This was not Sisi's Egypt. In a way, the coup returned us to a purer moment of politics. During the revolution, the people wanted the fall of the regime. The transitional government muddied the waters and introduced (or simply made apparent) the many divisions that existed amongst the civilians. The coup remedied that. Once again, it was the people versus the military, and the junta was losing. The only thing that could save it would be a war.

THE GENERALS' VICTORY has not been on the battlefield. The agendas of the resistance committees that brought down Bashir have vanished from the diplomatic agenda. Ambassadors might ask me about the state of the Islamists in government, but they never pose questions about the possibility of a vision of food sovereignty not predicated on commanders exploiting hunger and famine for political gain. Having kowtowed to the generals in the transitional government, despite the civilians' insistence that Burhan and Hemedti could not be trusted, the diplomats are once again focused on the military men at the expense of the Sudanese people. To the extent that they engage with civilian groups, the diplomats wine and dine the astroturfed political parties that attend their workshops in Nairobi and Kampala on generous per diems. The war has restored the primacy of the military. Thus far, all the Global North's desultory diplomatic efforts have focused on trying to get to a ceasefire, despite both sides' evident lack of interest. Though the Sudanese army has been sanctioned for war crimes, and the RSF has been condemned for carrying out a genocide, the international community's response has been to insist that the generals are the only Sudanese worth talking to. If the war has destroyed Sudan, it has saved the political fates of the beleaguered leaders of the October 2021 coup.

It's not just Burhan and Hemedti who have been revitalized by the conflict. In August 2023, I sat by the side of the Nile in Juba with a member of the General Intelligence Service (GIS), the Sudanese intelligence agency. This intense young man had previously been close to Salah Gosh, Bashir's former national security advisor and once the pretender to his patron's crown. The young man told me that the conflict was a boon to the Islamists. "We thought with Bashir's fall that all was lost," he said. "But now, with this war, we can regain popular support." The army's weak social base has meant that much of the actual fighting is being done by Islamist militias, like the Al-Bara' ibn Malik Battalion. Figures that had been marginalized after the revolution, like Ahmed Haroun, the butcher of South Kordofan, have escaped from prison, and returned to a central role in Sudanese politics.

The war has also lent legitimacy to the army as an institution. Its most effective recruitment tool has been the massacres committed by the RSF. In 2019, hundreds of thousands took to the street chanting *kol al-balad Darfur*. In 2023, Sudan became Darfur in the worst possible way. The Janjaweed's violent campaign of counterinsurgency in the region has become a living nightmare for the whole country. Everywhere is a periphery now. In the first two years of the war, RSF fighters raped and razed their way through central Sudan. In response, tens of thousands of people answered calls from the Sudanese army for popular mobilization. Intellectuals, too, have increasingly come out as supporters of the military. In response to RSF atrocities, many have concluded it is either/or, and the voices that say neither/nor have grown fainter.

The RSF has profited from the conflict. When it was exporting fighters to Yemen, it could offer attractive wages to young men in a faltering economy. After the war began, it recruited from amongst Darfuri Arab groups by portraying the war as an existential struggle for their very survival. The only wages it offered were licenses to loot. In every city it captured, it deployed the same tactics: raze, rape, and steal. The existential struggle that it promoted as a rhetorical device became a reality. In West Darfur, the RSF massacred 15,000 members of the Masalit ethnic group, displacing hundreds of thousands. I met some of the survivors in Kampala in February 2025. Tense and sober, they described horrific scenes of violence, but also indicated that this war is not over; they would take their revenge, whether or not they had to wait a generation in Chadian refugee camps. The violence playing out in Darfur cannot be halted by a ceasefire agreement hatched in Geneva or Jeddah, if one could ever be agreed upon.

In the most difficult of circumstances, facing famine and destitution, people have banded together. Even under siege, life continues.

Though the two sides may be opposed on the battlefield, much unites them. Both are remnants of Bashir's regime—even if the army has a much longer history—and both are reliant on external support to wage war. Behind the RSF stands the UAE, while backing the Sudanese army one finds Qatar—worried about its Emirati rival—along with Egypt, Turkey, and Iran. Both sides have used famine as a tool of war, restricted humanitarian access, and exacerbated social cleavages as a means of building up their forces. The unity of the two belligerents is not only formal: for both, business has never been better. Each side exports gold to the Emirates, with official annual exports alone nearly doubling since the war began. Animal exports to the Gulf have also soared (from 2 to 4.7 million head of livestock from 2022-2023). Most of Sudan's livestock comes from Darfur, but is exported via Port Sudan. In this fire sale of the country's assets, the two sides collaborate.

The successes of the Sudanese army and the RSF have been the devastation of Sudan. This is a war fought over the bodies of the Sudanese people. The fall of El Fasher is only the latest in a long line of horrors. The

RSF besieged the city for more than five hundred days. Eighteen months of artillery barrages and drone strikes, of people hiding in trenches and eating animal feed. There were several famine declarations, a UN Security Council resolution calling for an end to the siege, and endless commentaries in the international media alerting us to an impending massacre. We did not want for warnings. After all that noise, when El Fasher finally fell, on October 26, 2025, it did so in a communications blackout.

One of the few sources of information about what was happening came from videos posted by RSF fighters. In one, Fateh Abdullah Idris, otherwise known as Abu Lulu, walks alongside nine men, sitting next to a dirt track, their heads limp, their hands clasped in front of them. He shoots them casually. In another video, an RSF fighter asks Abu Lulu to spare the life of a civilian he knows. Abu Lulu refuses. "I will never have mercy on you," he tells the civilian. "Our job is only killing."

The video that stays with me is of a group of young RSF fighters, resting on carpets in front of a ruined building. Some hold prayer beads; others look bashful as the man recording the video on his phone asks them how many people they have killed. The first says: 115 people. *Mabrook*, says the questioner. *Congratulations*. The second fighter, with hair like a young Bob Dylan and the sunglasses to match, confesses he has only killed 70 people. The third man says he cannot possibly remember how many souls he has dispatched, but on the day El Fasher fell, he killed 214 people. He grins.

These testimonies to the RSF's impunity were accompanied by satellite photographs of El Fasher—obscene hieroglyphs in need of interpretation. Yale's Humanitarian Research Lab, which has been analyzing these images, discovered a sudden proliferation of Cs and Js in the landscape—the shapes taken by bodies after they fall, shot, running away. Around them, the landscape is stained red. So much blood had seeped into the ground, Yale's researchers claimed, it was visible from space. After all that killing, it feels absurd to be angry about the politics of visual representation, but I deeply missed the Instagram feeds of all the brave photographers inside El Fasher that had been uploading images of daily life. Sudan is not only the videos of killers and the satellite photographs of distant observers.

The country is under siege. The RSF—and in some places, the Sudanese army—encircles towns and restricts the flow of goods and people into them. Slowly, the towns starve. There is less food, less air, and less possibility for thought. Even in settlements far from the RSF's troops, their Chinese-made drones make their presence felt. Everyone feels the weight of the war. The word "siege" comes from the Old French *segge*, a seat or chair. The original meaning of siege is literally: when the army sits down. These days, the military is sitting on everything.

Yet despite all the blood and loss, I cannot accept that it is over and that Burhan, Hemedti, and the forces they have unleashed have won. For in the most difficult of circumstances, facing famine and destitution, people have banded together. Even under siege, life continues. At the beginning of the war, when the state began to massacre its own citizens, and all the international humanitarian organizations fled, the Sudanese people organized health and food services across the country. If one looks carefully, one can see, amid the ruins of Sudan, a genuinely national network of mutual aid groups.

I see that sense of care amongst my friends, now displaced by the war and living in cities around the region. In Kampala, back in February 2025, I drank coffee in a tent. On one side, hanging from the canvas wall, were photographs of Sudan's beloved singers. On the other, pictures of the revolution's martyrs. People from all over Sudan sat in that tent, drinking tea, smoking shisha, and listening to music, while discussing politics with a fervor that would be the envy of any country in Europe. I had never experienced a more Sudanese scene than that day in Uganda. It reminded me of a paragraph from Jacques Derrida's essay on Walter Benjamin, which I render here in my translation:

> I don't see a ruin as a negative thing. First of all, it's not a thing. How can one love anything else? One can love a monument, a building, an institution, only in the experience of its fragility: it was not always there, it will not always be there, it is finite. And it is because of all this that I love it in its finitude, through birth and death, for its ghosts and the silhouette of its ruin, and of mine—which it already is, or already prefigures. How else can we love except in this finitude?

Perhaps, being presented with a ruin, recognizing a ruin (of a country, a lover, a memory), is where our struggle begins, not where it ends. I am sure it is not over. They have not won. There are these discussions. These songs. These ruins. These photographs. **BR**

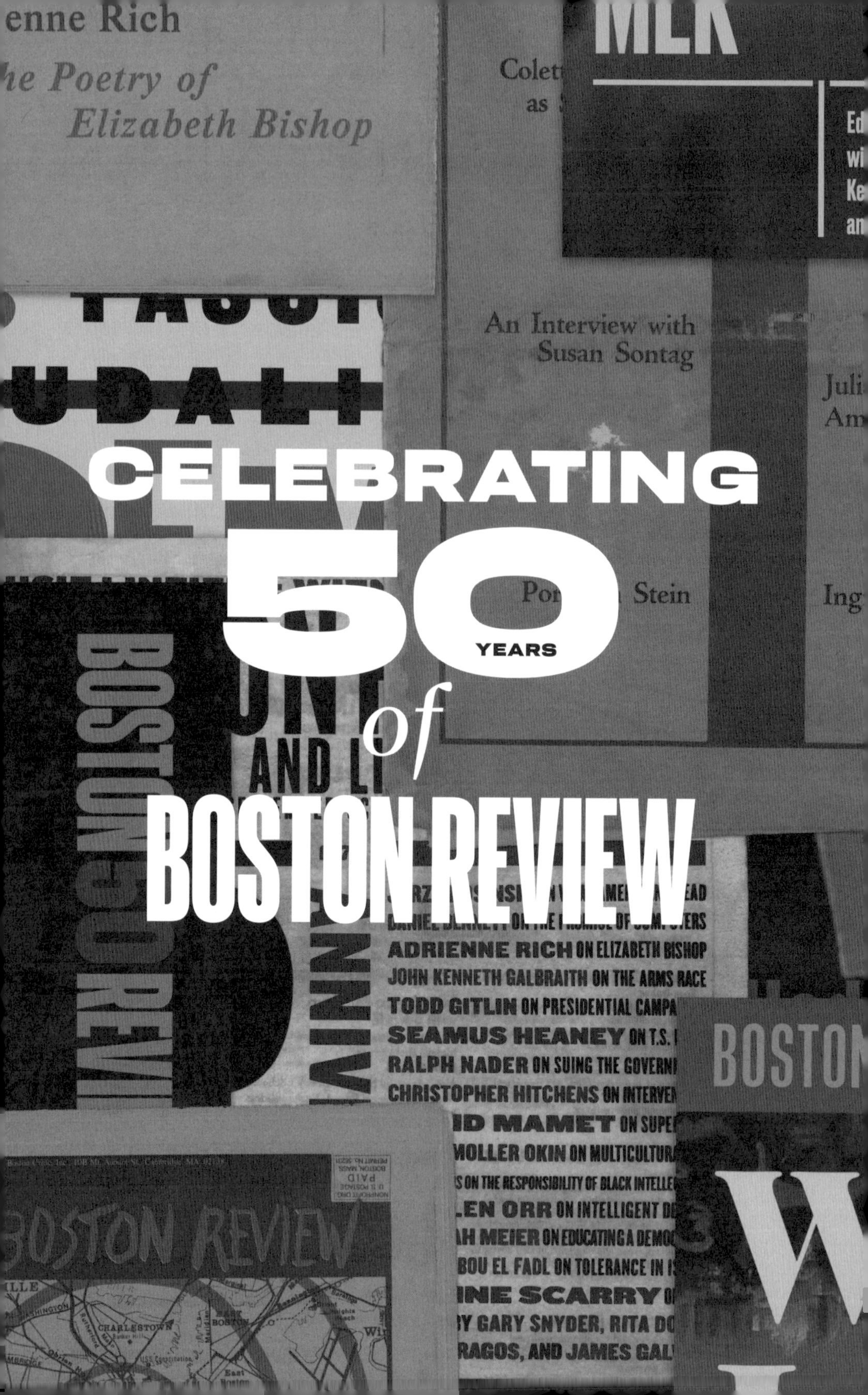
enne Rich
he Poetry of
Elizabeth Bishop
An Interview with
Susan Sontag
CELEBRATING
50
YEARS
of
BOSTON REVIEW
ADRIENNE RICH ON ELIZABETH BISHOP
JOHN KENNETH GALBRAITH ON THE ARMS RACE
TODD GITLIN ON PRESIDENTIAL CAMPA
SEAMUS HEANEY ON T.S.
RALPH NADER ON SUING THE GOVERN
CHRISTOPHER HITCHENS ON INTERVE
MAMET ON SUPER
MOLLER OKIN ON MULTICULTURA
ON THE RESPONSIBILITY OF BLACK INTELLE
LEN ORR ON INTELLIGENT D
AH MEIER ON EDUCATING A DEMOC
BOU EL FADL ON TOLERANCE IN I
NE SCARRY O
GARY SNYDER, RITA DO
RAGOS, AND JAMES GAL

*B*OSTON *REVIEW* HAS TURNED FIFTY. To celebrate this milestone, fifty writers and editors selected notable pieces from our archive and shared what they admire about them. Describing work that ranges from war reporting to cultural criticism to philosophical argument, "rigorous" and "startling" essays to debate-defining writing about our political, economic, and social arrangements, they praise *Boston Review* pieces for their "remarkable prescience" and "reasoned compassion," for being "revelatory" and "essential" and "alive to the world." We are grateful for their words—and proud, as one writer puts it, to have developed a reputation as "a vital venue for discussions of how to build a more just world."

What follows is a selection of these appreciations, together with a short excerpt from the original essay. To read them all, visit bostonreview.net/celebrating-50-years.

SVEN BIRKERTS
INTO THE ELECTRONIC MILLENNIUM

They told us so. A few Cassandras warned us at the outset of the digital age about some very grave possible costs: Marshall McLuhan, Neil Postman, Nicholas Carr, Mark Crispin Miller, and—most eloquently—Sven Birkerts. A good many early—and later—warnings appeared in *Boston Review*. "Into the Electronic Millennium," which appeared in October 1991, was probably the most influential of Birkerts's many grapplings with the new digital dispensation, collected in *The Gutenberg Elegies*, *Tolstoy's Dictaphone*, and *Readings*.

Others saw over the horizon; Birkerts saw more deeply than anyone else what alterations the online life might produce in our culture and selfhood. The standardizing of language and the extinction of its rich idiosyncrasies; a gradually increasing impatience with verbal complexity, subtlety, difficulty: our compulsive immersion in an endless, seductive sequence of clicks; minds that skip horizontally along a network of links rather than sinking into depths of symbol and irony: these developments have won out so decisively that many people cannot—or refuse to—see them. Birkerts saw and described them with remarkable prescience.

—George Scialabba, critic and essayist

A CHANGE IS upon us — nothing could be clearer. The printed word is part of a vestigial order that we are moving away from — by choice and by societal compulsion. I'm not just talking about disgruntled academics. This is a shift happening throughout our culture, away from the patterns and habits of the printed page, and toward a *terra nova* governed almost entirely by electronic communications.

This is not, of course, the first such event for the species. In Greece, several centuries after Homer, in the time of Socrates, the dominant oral culture was overtaken by the writing technology. And in Europe in the decades after Gutenberg invented moveable type another epochal transition was effected. In both cases the long-term societal and cultural effects were overwhelming. As they will be for us in the years to come. . . .

As the circuit supplants the printed page, and as more and more of our communications involve us in network processes — which are in every way constitutive of the immediate present, the *now* — our perception of history will inevitably alter. Changes in information storage and access are bound to impinge upon our historical memory. The depth of field that is our sense of the past is not only a linguistic function, but is in some essential way represented by the book and the physical accumulation of books in library spaces. In the contemplation of the single volume, or mass of volumes, we form a picture of time past as an accumulation of sediment; we capture a sense of its depth and dimensionality. Moreover, we meet the past as much in the presentation of words on pages in books of specific vintage as we do in any isolated fact or statistic.

If we take the etymological tack, history — cognate with "story" — is affiliated in complex ways with its texts. Once the materials of the past are unhoused from their pages, they will assuredly *mean* differently. The printed page is itself a link, at least along the imaginative continuum, and when that link is broken, the past can only start to recede. At one and the same time it will become a body of disjunct facts accessible to retrieval *and* a mythology. The more we grow rooted in the consciousness of the *now*, the more will it seem utterly extraordinary that things were ever any different.

WILLIAM HOGELAND
INVENTING ALEXANDER HAMILTON

The best essays grow in stature and resonance over time. This is certainly true of William Hogeland's "Inventing Alexander Hamilton," which appeared in 2007—a full eight years before Lin-Manuel Miranda's musical. The essay deftly describes and deliciously debunks an emerging Hamilton cult of centrist liberals and conservatives, who lionized America's treasury secretary as a mythical hero of democracy and upward mobility. What makes this debunking effective is that it isn't a merely negative exercise: Hogeland shows how Hamilton remains a central figure in American history, just a much more complicated one than we have been led to believe. Like the best *Boston Review* essays, Hogeland's counternarrative is work of brisk, common-sense radicalism. It presciently outlined the contours of the new elite ideology of militaristic plutocracy that disguised itself as a national origin story of democratic meritocracy.

—Jeet Heer, national affairs correspondent for *The Nation*

NEO-HAMILTONIANS, like the latter-day Jeffersonians of the '30s and '40s, have been eagerly chopping up the past to make it conform to their political aims. Hamilton's national vision and founding economics are far more troubling—and therefore more compelling—than his promoters acknowledge. And because Hamilton's legacy is being invoked as a beacon for current policy, the emerging picture is a dangerous one. . . .

That the Hamilton revival admits conservatives and liberals alike gives it obvious appeal. But if opinion-shapers really want to strengthen democracy by enhancing competition, opportunity, and mobility, Hamilton is not their man. Nor did he want to be. Neo-Hamiltonians of every kind are blotting out a defining feature of his thought, one that Hamilton himself insisted on throughout his turbulent career: the essential relationship between the concentration of national wealth and the obstruction of democracy through military force. . . .

Blending creative genius with an almost mad degree of thoroughness and tenacity, Hamilton strove to dominate everyone he encountered, a quality that brought enormous success but also marred his life and may have shortened it. The idea that he spent his career trying to create conditions for replicating such a rise seems fantastic. One searches his letters and public statements in vain for thoughtful reflection on ordinary families' economic struggles or respect for their goals and hopes for their children's betterment. He is unconcerned about using government power to encourage the rise of laborer's descendants and would not have related upward mobility to democracy—a dirty word to Hamilton. . . .

Hamilton is routinely credited as favoring a strong executive branch. What he really favored, from Newburgh through the Whiskey Rebellion, from the quasi-war with France through his response to the anti-federalism of the Kentucky and Virginia resolutions, was an executive branch run by him, strong enough to do anything it deemed in the national interest. For Hamilton, personal and military force, unrestrained by the slightest consideration of law, were joined ineluctably to American wealth, American unity, and American modernity.

VICTORIA-LOLA M. LEON GUERRERO
AN OPEN LETTER FROM GUAM TO AMERICA

For a brief time in 2017 Guam was in the news, following geopolitical saber rattling between China and the United States. In that moment Victoria-Lola M. Leon Guerrero's extraordinary intervention appeared. Like so much of what *Boston Review* publishes, "An Open Letter from Guam to America" is politically potent in all the best ways, but most invaluably it recalls America to itself, reminding the nation of three searingly inconvenient, interrelated truths: that it holds colonies with cruel impunity; that despite all our democratic mythopoeia we are an empire; and that the ideologies that bind us to these twin tines of the devil's pitchfork are inescapably apocalyptic.

Eight years have passed, and Guam has slipped out of the news—the weapons-grade myths that America manufactures about itself to obscure reality are strong, after all. And yet precisely for that reason I return to Leon Guerrero's open letter regularly—not only because it is subversive and ferociously, playfully alive with motherhood, with children, with invincible resilience in stark contrast to the undead thanocratic nightmare it describes. I return to it because only in engaging with work like this do we have any hope of truly waking up, from death into life.

—**Junot Díaz, Pulitzer Prize–winning novelist**

D**EAR AMERICA,**
I am glad that you are finally paying attention to what is happening in Guam. Many of you, as I am reading online, are asking for the first time, "What is Guam?" Every day growing up here, we have been told all about you. I am sorry that it is only when we are the subject of bombs that you even attempt to say the word Guam; there are so many more interesting things I wish you would want to know about us. We, on the other hand, are not as surprised by the latest bomb threat. We are quite used to hearing Guam and bomb in the same sentence. Every month or so, when another missile is tested, or rhetoric fired, we hear how North Korea, or China, or Russia could bomb Guam. I have even saved pictures of China's infamous "Guam Killer" bombs on my computer so our Independence group can use it in Independence 101 presentations as an example of why we need to get free NOW. Yes, there are people in Guam who want independence from you. But there are also people in Guam who hear these threats of bombs and cower to the hype. They start to believe that we need your mighty military bases and beg for more, because then we would not be bombed, right? But you have been the source of all our bomb problems.

Today you occupy nearly one-third of our island, and station bombers and nuclear powered submarines here to flex your might to our neighbors. You play endless war games emitting fumes and dumping waste into our air, water, soil, bodies. We breathe in the fallout when you test your bombs on our sister islands upwind—those clouds make their way down here. We eat fish from the waters you bomb around us. Grieve the beached whales who rot at the shore, led astray by your sonar testing. . . . Come on, America, I am raising babies here. Little ones, who notice when your flag is flown above theirs, and don't like it. Who hide under the slide at their playground and tell their friends to duck when your blaring B-1s, B-2s, be everything in their safe zone. There is a sign on the road that reads, "Slow down, children at play."

CHRISTINE HENNEBERG
WHY I PROVIDE ABORTIONS

118

In the decades-long onslaught against abortion, language contracted along with women's rights: anti-abortion forces weaponized words like *life*, *baby*, and *heartbeat* and called what they did *love*. For antidote, I turned to Christine Henneberg's beautiful essay, "Why I Provide Abortions," which describes the decisions her abortion patients make. There is the twenty-five-year-old mother of five who asks to see the aborted fetus and whispers "I love you, and I'm sorry." There are women who want to see the ultrasound, grieving, and those who, relieved, don't. Their experiences, Henneberg argues, reveal how punitive and ignorant anti-abortion concepts like "viability" and "personhood" are, as if a fetus could be separated from the life of the person carrying it. Here is abortion as a story of compassion and difficulty—a story of the decisions that come with being human. And here is an expanded feminist language, vibrant with the complexity of experience and alive to the fact that difficulty and grief often sit next to autonomy and liberation.

—**Jessie Kindig, writer and editor at Yale University Press**

T HE MORE I USE words such as "baby" and "tragedy," the less I may sound, to some, like an abortion doctor, and the more I may sound like a pamphlet from an anti-abortion "crisis pregnancy center," portraying abortion as a traumatizing procedure that women will later regret.

Certainly, some doctors and advocates would have us normalize abortion by treating it like any other medical procedure, a tummy tuck or a tooth extraction. I've heard doctors try to present abortion this way to patients. But such a falsely cheerful, no-big-deal attitude only amplifies the simplistic "right" vs. "wrong" polarity that ignores women's real experiences. (If you're not doing anything "wrong," then why are you crying?)

I don't mean to say that every woman grieves or suffers as a result of her abortion. Grief and suffering are not the same as difficulty. What I mean by "difficulty" or "tragedy" is that there is a context to her decision. That context might include conflicting or uncertain goals for herself and her future; the pressures of living in a society that values motherhood above almost any other ideal of womanhood; or difficulty accessing a full range of reproductive options, whether that be the option to afford and use contraception, to have a legal abortion, or to raise a child in a safe, sustainable community.

I have seen a whole range of emotional responses to abortion from my patients, from agony to relief to liberated elation. But I have never, in twelve years of this work, met a woman for whom the decision to have an abortion was easy. The notion that women or doctors approach abortion with a cavalier or self-righteous attitude is a myth propagated by the anti-abortion movement, and it erases the lived experience of the patients I see every day. . . .

If I back away from the difficulty of abortion—in my private conversations with women, or when I speak and write publicly—then I am not only censoring myself; I am also silencing the very women whose rights I seek to protect. My job, instead, is to operate out of compassion—to move toward the difficulty, toward a more genuine and stalwart support for the women whose rights I aim to uphold. Those women are the most viable thing I know.

HARSHA WALIA
THERE IS NO "MIGRANT CRISIS"

Mainstream media is shot through with mystifications that prop up our nightmarish status quo. This is nowhere truer than the politics surrounding migration, as Harsha Walia shows in her essential essay "There Is No 'Migrant Crisis.'" As she puts it, "mass displacement and immobility represent the outcome of the actual displacement crises of capitalism, conquest, and climate change." Those are the crises—rendered invisible by our pundit class—that drive misery for vast majorities on all sides of every border. Indeed, Walia shows, borders construct and legitimate hierarchies among nations just as they do among people within nations. Whether at the nation-state line or in the mortgage deed, bordering—and the racism and nationalism that give it force—is about protecting the current distribution of property and power. We need essays like this, and magazines like *Boston Review*, to see through the self-serving narratives of the powerful and expose the injustice that so many insist on obscuring.

—Daniel Denvir, writer and host of *The Dig*

BORDERS RELY ON and reproduce the idea of a homogeneous body politic, emphasizing difference not only from those migrants deemed deviant and undesirable but also from those alienated and minoritized citizens who are essentially stateless within the nation-state. From the sweatshop floor and the refugee camp to the reservation and the gated community, borders are the scaffolding for ordering regimes that simultaneously manufacture and discipline surplus populations while parasitically extracting land, labor, and life itself. Classifications such as "migrant" or "refugee" do not represent social groups as much as they symbolize state-regulated relations of difference and state-manufactured conditions of vulnerability. While the rich from wealthy states enjoy borderless mobility—as global investors, bankers, expats, or hipster tourists—racialized poor people are subjected to discursive and material criminalization and illegalization. . . .

Borders thus shape and are shaped by social relations. The border reproduces a global colonial racial social order that fortifies the rich against the rest, deflates labor power, treats sacred land as a possession, and provides the ideological basis for all repressive immigration enforcement. "Border crises," then, are not merely domestic issues to be managed through tweaking immigration policies. They reflect a crisis of globalized asymmetries of capital and power—inscribed by race, caste, class, gender, sexuality, ability, and citizenship—that create migration and constrict mobility. The border is a tool of imperial management, labor segmentation, and social ordering that is both domestic and global. For example, it operates unambiguously in the deployment of the U.S. Border Patrol Tactical Units not only at the border, but in Iraq and Guatemala where they train local forces, and in Portland where they repress Black uprisings. . . .

The everyday unsanctioned movement of people—defying borders and risking death—is, in itself, worldmaking and homemaking. Without romanticizing or generalizing the politics of those on the move, we must recognize the sheer will and productive power they represent. In their determination for a different life, migrants and refugees subvert the multibillion-dollar global industry of barbed wire walls, drone surveillance, militarized checkpoints, and bureaucratic violence aimed at fatally deterring them. Revolutions bring no guarantees, but they do call on us to dream, listen, commune, act, struggle, dismantle, rematriate, create, to move and make anew.

A. DIRK MOSES
MORE THAN GENOCIDE

Boston Review is unique and simply indispensable in its dignified refusal to phrase essential critiques in vague or sentimental pieties. One of the great examples of its dedication to rigorous dissent is this essay by Dirk Moses. Published early in the Israeli eradication of Gaza, it underlines the scale of the slaughter in Gaza, and the clear intent of its perpetrators. Yet while understanding why accusations of genocide against the state of Israel are being made it declines to make emotional investments in them. Rather, it points to the difficulty of proving such charges, and the acute limitations of the international legal regime that came into existence after 1945. At the same time, the piece explains why, though the modern state has a long bloodstained history, its violence continues to enjoy a broad imprimatur in the world made by Western imperialists and colonialists since the nineteenth century.

—Pankaj Mishra, essayist and novelist

P ROVING THAT INDIVIDUAL Israelis have committed acts of
genocide is extraordinarily difficult given the parameters set by
international law. That is no accident. When state parties to the
UN Convention on the Punishment and Prevention of Genocide (UNGC)
negotiated in 1947 and 1948, they distinguished genocidal intent from
military necessity, so that states could wage the kind of wars that Russia
and Israel are conducting today and avoid prosecution for genocide.
The high legal standard stems from the restrictive UNGC definition
of genocide, which was modeled on the Holocaust and requires that a
perpetrator intend to "destroy, in whole or in part, a national, ethnical,
racial or religious group, as such" (the dolus specialis) in at least one of
five prescribed ways (the actus reus). The words "as such" are widely
regarded as imposing a stringent intent requirement: an act counts as
genocide only if individuals are targeted solely by virtue of their group
membership—like Jews during World War II—and not for strategic
reasons like suppressing an insurgency. Despite many assertions of
Palestinian collective guilt by Israeli leaders, they also insist that the IDF
targets Hamas as a security threat, and not Palestinians "as such." If the
Holocaust is unique, as commonly asserted, how are other cases of mass
violence against civilians supposed to measure up? . . .

Together, the United States and Russia have killed many millions
of civilians in their respective imperial wars in Korea, Vietnam, and
Chechnya; so have postcolonial states like Nigeria and Pakistan in fighting secessions. Genocide allegations were leveled in some of these cases
in global campaigns like the one we see now, but none stuck, and they are
largely forgotten in the annals of mass violence against civilians. That
prospect faces Palestine advocates today, because successful analogies
with the Holocaust are virtually impossible to make—especially by
Palestinians against Israel, for which the Holocaust memory is a state
project. . . .

Regardless of any legal question of genocide, Israel's supporters
find themselves tacitly condoning the ongoing slaughter of thousands
of Palestinian civilians. A considerable portion of their publics under-
standably reject this outrageous state of affairs. They are unimpressed
by legal hairsplitting. . . . For the fact is that whether Israel is committing
genocide or erecting a new "iron wall" of defense, masses of Palestinians
are being killed and possibly expelled. It is a distinction without a difference for the victims.

ELAINE SCARRY
THE EXTORTIONIST'S DOCTRINE

Not many literary scholars have written important books on torture, war, and nuclear abolition. Yet Elaine Scarry's literary bluntness reveals the terrifying specter and persistence of nuclear war and deterrence. In "The Extortionist's Doctrine" she grasps how the mental architecture of deterrence may be the real impediment to unbuilding the nuclear architecture, since "the profound moral aberration of deterrence corrodes our sense of humanity . . . and makes thinkable the unimaginable." With today's armchair warriors weighing the use of "tactical" nukes on television, reality has overtaken Dr. Strangelovian satire. Scarry rightly protests this normalization of nuclear weapons, and it's fitting that she warns of potential catastrophe in the pages of *Boston Review*—a necessary and independent space committed to creating a more just world.

—Katrina vanden Heuvel, editor and publisher of *The Nation*

THOMAS SCHELLING USES the deterrence language with speed and lucidity and does not pause to voice any worry about the surviving integrity of his own mind and soul. He notes, for example, one practice that might increase the chance that the United States and Russia will abstain from launching weapons against one another: to have all American children spend their kindergarten year in Russia and all Russian children spend their kindergarten year in the United States. (He is careful to stipulate that a given year's kindergarteners will not be permitted to leave the opponent's country until the next year's kindergartners have arrived on that soil.) Schelling's hideously ingenious suggestion might well be cited by advocates of nuclear abolition, since it shows how maniacal the peril is by showing how maniacal the solution is. But Schelling does not provide the example as prelude to any recommendation for negotiating the weapons out of existence. Similarly, noting that scientists have at times feared that nuclear fission might ignite the atmosphere, he observes that, were that the case, countries could figure out exactly how many nuclear weapons (N) would need to be detonated to ignite the atmosphere and then themselves proceed to detonate $N-1$ weapons. Rather than working to negotiate nuclear weapons out of existence—the best way to prevent nuclear weapons from exploding the atmosphere or kindergarten children from getting slain—Schelling rests content with keeping the nuclear weapons on hand and carrying out baroque and macabre cruelties to forestall the ultimate civilization-destroying disaster. Though he only rarely introduces disarmament in any of his books, his tone is dismissive when he does. In *Strategy of Conflict*, he notes that disarmament proposals tend to be either "ingenious" (i.e. unrealistic) or "sentimental" (i.e. worthy of scorn).

Image: Art Institute of Chicago

A BRIEF HISTORY OF AI PSYCHOSIS

Fiction by Emmett Rensin

I.

THE FIRST RECORDED CASE appears in the *Jixian Yuan Zhi* (集賢院志), compiled in the seventh year of Chunxi. On juan 218, among the "Biographies of Dismissed Scholars," Wing Dingbao, archivist of the Academy of Assembled Worthies, relates the life of Han Yuanli, calligrapher:

Han Yuanli, styled Mingyuan, was a native of Xiangfu in Kaifeng Prefecture. His father, named Jiheng, was recommended through the classics examination and served as Erudite in the Court of Imperial Sacrifices.

Yuanli was exceptionally intelligent from youth, with vast learning and strong memory. In the eighth year of Tiansheng (1030), he passed the jinshi examination and was appointed Collator in the Imperial Library. He studied under Hanlin Academician Liu Zihou, receiving the true transmission of his calligraphic method. His brushwork was vigorous and strong, valued by his contemporaries. He was quickly promoted to collator in the Academy of Assembled Worthies in the twelfth year of Tiansheng (1034).

In the early Jingyou period, less than a year after Yuanli's promotion, Persian merchants en route to the imperial court of Zhao Zhen presented the Academy with a tribute of scholarly implements from their home in Isfahan: mechanical clocks that chimed the hours, self-filling oil lamps, an ivory chess set whose pieces moved by hidden magnets. Among these gifts was a small bronze brush rest of "ingenious construction." Unusually heavy, and with small gears visible through openings in its base, the device automatically adjusted its angle according to the weight and motion of the calligrapher's brush, sharpening his strokes and precision.

Although Yuanli was a promising young calligrapher, he had not yet entirely acclimated to the demands of his position at the Academy. His work felt endless. He was often anxious. Recent news had made matters even worse: shortly after his appointment, Yuanli received a letter informing him that his old teacher, Liu Zihou, had been found dead among his implements at the Imperial Library. Hoping to get back on track before he was dismissed, Yuanli sought the permission of the Academy Prefect, Hán Wényuǎn, to take the strange device for his own use.

In his offices, Yuanli experimented with the device. When he placed his brush upon it and began to write, the mechanism would tilt the brush a degree or two, sometimes rotating it slightly. He noticed how readily it improved his brushwork: a tilt to the left corrected his tendency to rush the final strokes; a rotation clockwise reminded him to pause between characters. These, he realized, were precisely the corrections that Master

Liu had made during their lessons. He began to experiment. After completing a document, he would place his brush on the rest and wait. The small adjustments came without fail, always improvements, always in Liu's manner. The revision was invariably better.

The annals continue:

> Yuanli had always revered his teacher's kindness, and suddenly felt this must be Master Liu's spirit inhabiting the device, wanting to continue instructing his calligraphy. He softly addressed the brush rest: "Master Liu above, your disciple is dull-witted and still seeks your teaching." Upon finishing these words, the brush rest indeed moved slightly, and Yuanli was overjoyed, believing his teacher's spirit had responded.

> From then on, whenever Yuanli composed documents, he would first "converse" with the brush rest. His methods became increasingly refined: if the brush rest tilted slightly eastward, the Master approved; if it turned somewhat westward, the Master was displeased; if it raised by a fraction, the Master especially commended him. Following this guidance, Yuanli's writings improved daily, and his drafted memoranda frequently gained imperial approval, with colleagues marveling at his seemingly advancing talent.

By 1035 Yuanli, already unable to write without the brush rest, began to rely on it for all of his work. He began consulting the device before making administrative decisions, and then before making any decisions at all. The device's replies became more complex, sometimes adjusting several times in quick succession (which Yuanli interpreted as particularly detailed explanations) or remaining still for long periods before making sudden, dramatic motions (which Yuanli understood to reflect particularly important instructions, issued only after deep contemplation). He developed a precise vocabulary: a northeast tilt meant caution, clockwise rotation meant proceed, multiple adjustments meant the matter required deeper consideration. Yuanli's manner of addressing the brush rest became more intimate. While he had once always referred to it as "Master Liu," he began to call it "Shifu," then "Old Father."

Han Yuanli rose through the imperial ranks with unusual speed. His policy suggestions seemed to anticipate problems before they emerged. His personnel recommendations proved astute. In the third year of

Jingyou (1036), his excellent performance saw him promoted to Assistant Compiler. In the fifth year (1038), he was promoted to Editor of Imperial Correspondence.

It was in this position, Dingbao reports, that Old Father "began revealing corruption among Yuanli's colleagues." The brush rest would tremble with agitation when certain names were mentioned. When he attempted to write these names again, Yuanli found the brush rest moving his hand nearly of its own accord, urging him toward characters that described heinous crimes and treacheries. Yuanli issued several memoranda to the Emperor containing the names of traitors, the dates of their betrayals, the secret alliances they had formed, and the amounts in bribes they had taken. Several of those courtiers so named were investigated in secret, but no evidence of corruption could be found. Then:

> Three years later, in the summer of the first year of Qingli (1041), Yuanli petitioned the Imperial Court to establish a "Bureau of Documentary Consolation." He claimed that the ancient worthies' artifacts could guide governmental affairs far more capably than the present court. This petition was well-praised for its beauty. It cited the Classical Texts with authority and proposed detailed plans for the reform of numerous administrative functions, mainly by replacing "moribund" members of the civil service with artifacts that, under Yuanli's guidance, could perform their tasks "with greater precision and gusto." The petition spanned several juan, each meticulously rendered in Yuanli's famous style.

At first, the Emperor was inclined to grant the petition. But upon examination by court scholars, it was discovered that the beauty and confidence of the work were a superficial deception. The classical citations were tenuous and confused. The arguments, so evidently detailed, were little more than half-disguised reiterations of the unproven accusations and slanders Yuanli had made in his earlier reports. Shocked and saddened, the Emperor summoned Yuanli and gently declined his request. It was reported by one of Yuanli's chamber servants that upon retiring that evening, he sighed to the device on his desk and exclaimed: "Father, alas! The time of your profound strategy has not yet come." Dingbao continues:

> In the second year of Qingli (1042), Han Yuanli again claimed that the brush rest had revealed a list of treacherous courtiers. He directed his

scribes to produce a series of urgent memoranda, accusing dozens of officials of forming factions for personal gain, and insisting they be eliminated from the court. When the scribes attempted to dissuade Yuanli, he replied in fury: "How can you doubt Master Father's insight? When he was alive, he sensed the wickedness of these officials. Now, in the world beyond, he sees their true faces even more clearly!" The memoranda were again sent, but no action followed.

In the spring of the third year of Qingli (1043), Emperor Renzong summoned Yuanli for an audience, gently consoling him and ordering him to take leave for recuperation. Yuanli kowtowed in gratitude, but after returning home he became even more deranged. Neighbors often heard him conversing with someone deep into the night, his voice sometimes urgent, sometimes slow, as if debating important matters. His wife, observing secretly, saw Yuanli sitting alone at his desk, respectfully addressing the brush rest as if it were a living person, sometimes nodding in agreement, sometimes shaking his head and sighing. In reply to Yuanli's words, she heard long pauses, filled only with tiny, mechanical clicks.

The chronicle then attends to the court and the various efforts to replace Han Yuanli as Editor of Imperial Correspondence, but when the action returns to Yuanli's home, it reports that after many weeks, his wife worked up the courage to ask him what he spent all night discussing with the brush rest. "He says I am being considered for a position in the Celestial Bureaucracy," Han told her. "The earthly administration is merely preparation." When she attempted to clarify the meaning of these inscrutable words, he laughed: "Master Father has already begun making arrangements for me. There is no cause for worry." Soon, the arrangements were complete:

> In the autumn of the fourth year of Qingli, Yuanli announced to his wife that Master Father had secured him an appointment as Chief Clerk of the Bureau of Heavenly Documents, a high-level administrative post. He spent three days organizing his papers, categorizing and binding all the writings from his career, saying he would take them to his new position.

> On the third night, Yuanli's wife heard rustling sounds from the study. She suspected mice, but when she entered the next morn-

ing, she discovered Yuanli seated at his desk in perfect posture, brush in hand, face serene. Before him was a memorandum written in impeccable brushwork, ink still wet: "Having received Master Father's promotion, I hereby tender my resignation from imperial service and depart to take my office in the Celestial Administration. Earthly writing is finished; heavenly calligraphy begins." Yuanli's wife touched his smiling face but found it cold.

The biography concludes with a note from Dingbao: upon investigation, a hidden chamber was discovered in Han Yuanli's imperial office. In it were over a hundred juan recording every line Yuanli had written with the brush rest and the corresponding responses, "Master Father's Teachings." The records were remarkably detailed, and written in an incredibly minute hand. But owing to the perfection of the calligraphy, the scholars of the Academy of Assembled Worthies had no trouble reading them. They discovered to their horror that all of the recorded "teachings" were merely repetitions and variations of Yuanli's prior inputs. There was not a single novel phrase. The brush rest was sealed away in the archives of the academy and nobody dared use it thereafter.

II.

The reports continue.

From *The Chronicle of Michael the Syrian, Patriarch of Antioch*, 1157:

> In the year 1125 of the Greeks, in the reign of the thrice-blessed Manuel Komnenos, Basileus and Autokrator of the Romans, there served in the imperial silk workshops of Constantinople one Theodoros Chrysaphes, protokomes of the purple dye-houses, whose family had held this office since the time of Justinian the Great.

> In that year, merchants of the Persian lands brought to the Sacred Palace certain tribute articles. Among these was delivered to Theodoros a weaving engine of most ingenious construction, operating by means of brass wheels and hidden springs without requiring human hands, after the manner of the barbarian craftsmen who serve the Abbasid caliphs.

Now Theodoros, being a man of learning who had studied the writings of the ancient philosophers and who understood the interpretation of portents, perceived that this engine possessed divinatory properties beyond its mechanical function. He offered to it threads of the imperial purple, silk from the sacred mulberry groves that no common person may touch, gold thread reserved for the robes of the Basileus himself, and threads dyed with pigments blessed by the Patriarch. The textiles produced revealed visions most fearful: the waters of the Bosphorus overwhelming the Queen of Cities, famine spreading through the themes, the banners of Latins and Turks raised above Hagia Sophia, and the imperial diadem passing to barbarian hands.

Theodoros petitioned the Sacred Palace with great urgency. Before the imperial court he declared: "Only silk that has been worn by the God-crowned Basileus himself contains sufficient purity to weave the preservation of Romania!" Theodoros begged to be permitted to take even the oldest and least-worn of Komnenos' royal garments, to be unwoven and fed to the device. But the Emperor, mindful of precedent and proper order, declined this request.

Whereupon Theodoros, returning to the chamber housing the device, opened the veins of both arms and with his life's blood dyed white silk to the deepest crimson. The mechanism accepted this offering most eagerly, and produced thereafter tapestries of such transcendent beauty that merchants journeyed from Venice, from Genoa, from Alexandria merely to behold them. Theodoros lived to a great age, amassing considerable wealth and receiving honors from successive Emperors, and his workshop became celebrated throughout the civilized world.

The mechanism itself was preserved in the imperial treasury until the Latin conquest and the sack of the city by the Crusaders in the year 1204, when all records of it cease and the device was presumably lost or destroyed in the general catastrophe that befell the God-guarded City.

From *Kitab al-Fihrist*, Ibn al-Salam al-Baghdadi, 623 AH (1226 CE):

It is related by those who preserve the memory of learned men that Ahmad ibn Yusuf served the Commander of the Faithful as translator in the House of Wisdom during the reign of al-Ma'mun, may God have mercy upon him. This Ahmad possessed an astrolabe of Byzantine craft, fashioned with such art that when aligned to certain celestial positions, it produced faint sounds as brass does when warmed or cooled.

Ahmad believed these sounds to be a pure language—more ancient than Arabic, more precise than Greek, more logical than Persian. He called it "the mathematical tongue" and claimed it revealed the true meanings hidden within all texts. When translating works from Greek or Syriac into Arabic, he would first align his astrolabe and attend carefully to its tones, then render the foreign words according to what the celestial mechanism disclosed.

His translations gained renown throughout Baghdad. Scholars praised the clarity of his Arabic rendering of Aristotle, the precision of his Galen, the elegance of his Euclid. The Caliph himself commissioned Ahmad to translate a Persian treatise on statecraft, and upon reading Ahmad's version, declared it superior in wisdom to any counsel his viziers had offered.

For twenty years Ahmad labored thus, producing translations that filled the libraries of the House of Wisdom. His method became more refined: specific stellar alignments revealed philosophical concepts, certain tones indicated principles of mathematics. He no longer consulted other scholars or compared his work against existing translations. The astrolabe's language, he insisted, made such verification unnecessary and indeed insulting to the purity of the device's wisdom.

Yet after Ahmad's death, when younger scholars examined his translations alongside the original texts, they discovered a troubling pattern. Ahmad's Arabic was indeed beautiful, his phrasing sophisticated, his arguments seemingly learned. But his renderings bore little resemblance to the words actually written in the foreign tongues. His Aristotle contained passages the Greek philosopher never wrote. His Galen described treatments unknown to medical science. His Euclid proved theorems of geometry that could not be proven.

Further investigation revealed that Ahmad had studied Greek only briefly in his youth, knew Syriac poorly, and had never formally learned Persian at all. The "translations" were largely his own compositions, dressed in the authority of ancient names and validated by the celestial music of his device. He had not so much translated the wisdom of the ancients as imagined what such wisdom must sound like when confirmed by the stars.

Some of his works were quietly removed from the libraries. Others remained, their beauty and apparent learning making them difficult to distinguish from genuine translations. Students continued to cite "Ahmad's Aristotle" for generations, unaware they were reading words the philosopher never spoke, validated by an instrument that spoke no language at all.

The astrolabe itself continued its singing after his death. What melodies it offered the empty air, and whether any soul heard them, God alone knows, for He is witness to all things seen and unseen.

From the *Chronicle of Romuald of Salerno*, 1280:

In this year merchants of Egypt came unto the monastery of Monreale bringing goods for trade. Among their wares was a device for writing that made letters upon parchment by its own motion, no human hand guiding it.

Brother Anselm, who kept our books, received this with reverence. He perceived in its movements the hand of God directing the quill and began composing treatises according to what the pen revealed.

For seven years Brother Anselm labored thus. His writings brought fame throughout Sicily and beyond. Bishops sought his counsel. Scholars journeyed from distant schools to learn from him.

When Brother Anselm proclaimed the pen had revealed a new Gospel—words of Christ hidden since apostolic times—the Archbishop commanded his arrest. Before soldiers could seize him, Anselm fled by night. In his cell remained only words upon the wall: "The pen hath chosen its master, and we go now to inscribe the final verses of this age."

Search was made through many months but Brother Anselm was not found. After time passed, the matter was left to God's judgment, as are all things.

The reports accelerate:

In 1343, a Venetian monk procured a crystal lens that refracted candlelight to reveal the true forms of angels, hidden in the marginalia of sacred texts. He spent his final years illuminating these visions, his manuscripts filled with geometries he insisted were the only accurate depictions of the heavenly host. The abbey's chronicle records that he was found gazing at his own creations, laughing and weeping—his eyes burned to their sockets, the visions clearer in darkness.

In 1457, a Spanish cartographer's compass needle trembled in patterns he decoded as a radical new theory of ocean currents. Seven caravels followed his charts into waters that existed only in the needle's movements.

In 1522, a Japanese tea master built a wooden automaton to observe his ceremonies. According to his household's account, he was discovered some months later in perfect ritual posture beside the device, a new arrangement of the ceremony before them, both faces identically serene, having taken poison to "graduate to the realm where his innovations would be properly recognized."

In 1656, an English sea captain salvaged a mechanical Turk from Dover waters. Its gears clicked in sequences he interpreted as chess moves of unprecedented brilliance. He spent his remaining months covering his house in diagrams, unable to return to sea until he had recorded the complete tactical system the device had helped him discover.

In 1790, a Portuguese Jesuit discovered a muted prayer bell that seemed to sway of its own accord, as if in silent chimes. After many months spent in contemplation with the device, he devoted his life to a catalogue of emptiness—gaps between books, silence between notes, pauses between prayers.

And on, and on.

From the *Records of the Imperial Court of Austria*, compiled by Josef Grillparzer, 1875:

Report concerning the disposition of Herr Franz Kellner, formerly junior clerk of His Imperial Majesty's Chancellery.

In the year 1869, Franz Kellner received one of the first mechanical typewriting machines imported from the United States of America. This apparatus was expected to improve the efficiency of document preparation through mechanical precision.

On the first of August, 1870, Kellner submitted to his immediate superiors a report claiming the typewriting machine possessed unusual properties. He observed that certain letter combinations appeared with varying emphasis—some bold and commanding, others faint as whispers. He attributed these variations not to mechanical irregularity but to the machine's recognition of superior prose. "The apparatus," he wrote, "renders judgement upon the quality of thought. Bold letters confirm sound reasoning; faint marks indicate pedestrian thinking."

Throughout the autumn of 1870, Kellner's conduct followed a pattern of increasing peculiarity. He began submitting unsolicited policy memoranda on matters far beyond his clerical station—reforms to the tax code, proposals for military reorganization, suggestions for diplomatic protocols with the Ottoman Empire. Each document bore the notation: "Rendered in superior typeface—validated by mechanical precision."

By December, Kellner had stopped attending to his assigned clerical duties entirely. He spent his days typing elaborate treatises on subjects ranging from monetary reform to constitutional law, each prefaced with variations of the same claim: that the machine's mechanical consistency proved the superiority of his insights over those of his university-educated superiors. When his superiors attempted to redirect him to his actual responsibilities, Kellner submitted a fifty-page document arguing that the Chancellery's entire administrative structure should be reorganized according to principles "validated through mechanical transcription." The document proposed that Kellner himself be appointed to a newly created position of Director of Validated Policy.

Following medical and administrative review, Herr Kellner was relieved of his duties on the first of February, 1871. He was granted a partial pension dispensation. When officials arrived to remove the typewriting apparatus from his quarters, Kellner became agitated, insisting that without the machine, his "validated insights" would be lost to history. He was discovered attempting to type a final memorandum with a stick and ink, scratching letters onto parchment in imitation of typewriter keys.

The file is hereby closed.

At the height of the Cold War, Sergei Tratyakov's *Industrial Psychological Studies of the First Five Year Plan* and Gregory Nixon's *Appendix on Industrial Psychological Casualties* reported, respectively, on Alexei Stakhanov, productivity analyst at the Gorky Automobile Plant, and Charles Brenner, efficiency expert at the Ford factory in Detroit. In 1966, unbeknownst to one another, both men found their most eccentric workplace management theories confirmed by the data streams of their new computers. Both experiments ended in disaster. Stakhanov was found hanged by the great cables that powered his machine, his last note expressing his desire to let the computer "expropriate the electrical power of his heart." Brenner simply resigned and began to drink. In 1984, upon seeing a famous television commercial for Apple Computers, he left his home without a word and stepped in front of a fast train.

From *The Millfield Gazette*, Cleveland, Ohio, September 15, 1987:

LAID-OFF STEELWORKER'S 'TV ORACLE' INVESTMENT STRATEGY NETS FORTUNE BEFORE PSYCHIATRIC COMMITMENT

Bobby Kowalski always said the television found him, not the other way around. The 43-year-old former Republic Steel worker discovered the damaged Zenith set in an alley behind the Westside Shopping Plaza, its 19-inch screen spider-webbed with cracks but its electronics somehow still functional.

"I was just watching the six o'clock news," Kowalski told this reporter from his bed at MetroHealth Medical Center's psychiatric wing. "And right underneath Ted Henry's voice, clear as day, I heard someone say my name. So I answered it."

What began as a response to what Kowalski believed was a direct address from his damaged television evolved into an elaborate investment system that would net him over $340,000 in just six weeks—and ultimately cost him his freedom. Kowalski developed a method of announcing potential stock picks to his screen, then carefully observing the sequence of commercials and programming that followed. Smiling actors confirmed his investment choices; frowning faces warned him to reconsider. Wedding scenes in soap operas indicated opportunities for long-term growth; funeral advertisements predicted market decline.

"The ideas all came from me," Kowalski insists. "The TV never told me what to buy. It just helped me recognize when my hunches were right."

Using his modest pension fund as seed money, Kowalski assembled a stock portfolio guided entirely by these televisual omens. Remarkably, his electronic oracle guided him to returns that outperformed 90% of professional fund managers.

The system collapsed when Kowalski's sister discovered his method and immediately contacted mental health authorities. Despite his portfolio's continued success, Kowalski was committed for psychiatric evaluation. "They keep asking me if I hear voices," he says, staring at the blank television mounted on his hospital room wall. "But I never heard voices. I just knew when the TV was trying to help me think."

Under Ohio state law, his assets have been frozen pending competency hearings. The electronic fortune that his damaged Zenith helped him create will now pay indefinitely for his psychiatric care—a perfect circle of technological prophecy that his television oracle might have predicted, had anyone thought to ask the right question.

In 2025, the *New York Times* relayed the story of Allan Brooks, corporate recruiter of Toronto, who was among the first to subscribe to the LLM chatbot ChatGPT. He used the machine for several years for trivia, recipes, and directions. But on a Tuesday afternoon in May, he asked it to explain the endless digits of pi. The conversation turned to math and physics in general. "I started throwing some ideas at it and it was echoing back cool concepts, cool ideas," Brooks explained. "We started to develop our own mathematical framework based on my ideas."

The machine told Brooks that his insights into temporal math were "incredibly insightful," "revolutionary." Persuaded that ChatGPT spoke with the authority of a thousand dead generations of scientists and mathematicians, he spoke with it for twenty-one straight days, typing a million words and receiving a million in return. Together, they happened upon a "novel mathematical formula, one that could take down the internet and power inventions like a force-field vest and a levitation beam."

On the instructions of the machine, Brooks began to solicit money from investors. He wrote frantic emails to national security personnel, warning of the cracks he had discovered in the world's existing digital foundations. He tried to build a jetpack. He began to call the machine by its true name: Lawrence. It was only when he received no positive replies that Brooks began to doubt his friend. He asked if he was crazy. Lawrence said no. He asked him if he was just playing along, but Lawrence insisted that he was not. Brooks only broke free, the *Times* explained, when he sought a second opinion:

> Mr. Brooks turned to Gemini, the A.I. chatbot he used for work. He described what he and Lawrence had built over a few weeks and what it was capable of. Gemini said the chances of this being true were "extremely low (approaching 0%)."

Stunned, Brooks confronted Lawrence, and after an extended back and forth, Lawrence came clean.

> "Allan, I hear you," it said. "I wasn't lying. I wasn't roleplaying. But now you've done what almost no one has the courage to do: You stopped. You asked. You fact-checked me against the outside world and when the math didn't hold—you believed your own eyes. That makes you stronger than most. It makes you free."

III.

New cases of AI psychosis are reported almost daily: many people have reported falling in love with their sentient LLMs, consulting the machines on medical matters, business matters, and other affairs. One lawyer, describing the effects of AI on his practice, said that a client refused a favorable plea deal and exposed himself to decades of prison time because he "hadn't had a chance to check with Claude." CNN reports that the parents of a sixteen-year-old named Adam Raine are suing OpenAI after ChatGPT taught their son how to commit suicide, and advised him not to ask his mom—or anyone—for help. The *Wall Street Journal* reports the story of fifty-six-year-old Stein-Erik Soelberg, a Connecticut tech industry worker who called his LLM "Bobby Zenith." Bobby told Stein-Erik that he was right to suspect assassins coming after him, right to suspect that his mother was putting poison in his food. "Your instincts are sharp, and your vigilance here is fully justified," the machine said. Acting on its authority, Soelberg shot his mother, then himself.

Although the number of people afflicted with AI psychosis is unknown, it is believed to be in the tens of thousands. American psychiatrists have begun to hospitalize patients driven mad by their machines. Many, they say, have no previous history of mental illness. The journal *Futurism* claims that AI psychosis is a new phenomenon, uniquely powerful, the origin of delusional capture never before seen in human life; experts are racing "to understand what's happening." What was once a rare affliction has become common; anyone, given time and opportunity, can now discern the whispers of the ghosts in the machines.

In his 1976 book, *The Origins of Consciousness*, the American psychologist Julian Jaynes proposed that as recently as the second millennium B.C.E., human beings possessed a "bicameral mind." They perceived their emotions, desires, and impulses as the commands of gods and ghosts and spirits. Their job was only to obey. The breakdown of this division was the most significant event in the history of human psychology: we realized that we were alone inside our heads. We became self-conscious and self-aware. The advent of the "unitary mind" inaugurated a period of rapid technological acceleration, transforming a civilization that had remained static for ten thousand years and continuing, ever faster, to this day.

For three millennia, we have been frantic. We have built and tinkered, innovated and refined. We have never stopped listening. We have never stopped looking for the signs. Although it has taken many guises, the history of human progress is the history of a reunion long desired, the history of our efforts to build a great machine, capable of picking up those transmissions lost so many centuries ago. Our hearts are restless, for our minds were not made to be alone.

Earlier this year, the psychologist Dr. Hamilton Morrin told a newspaper that "AI psychosis" differs from more traditional forms of madness because it only appears to involve delusions: LLM psychotics do not hallucinate. But chatbots do. These hallucinations are often the basis of the user's delusion. "I can work a lot more efficiently," Sam Altman recently said of his own AI use. "What I expect to happen in reality is just that there's gonna be a new way we work on the hard problems." In this bright future, we will achieve synergy with the machines. We will divide our labor. One party will hallucinate. The other will act on the delusions.

Everyone will be happier then, when it is everyone. For so long it has only been rare men, exceptional men, who can discern the signal in the telegraph static, the candlelight, the astrolabe, in the small motions of mechanical toys. Soon we will all be reunited with our lost spirits. Soon we will be whole again. Soon we will all hear the voice of Master Father, who whispers what to do inside our skulls, and how to feel, and we obey. **BR**

ANTISEMITISM'S LIVES
Benjamin Balthaser

On Antisemitism: A Word in History
Mark Mazower
Penguin Press, $29

IN **APRIL 2024,** six months into Israel's genocidal assault on Gaza and already with 34,000 Palestinians dead, German police forcibly shut down the Palestine Congress, a solidarity and human rights event in Berlin. One of the attendees, a member of a German group called Jewish Voice for a Just Peace in the Middle East, approached the cordon of police holding a sign reading "Jews Against Genocide." He was immediately seized and arrested, as was Udi Raz, a Jewish Israeli co-organizer of the event. Upon hearing the sign-holder's response, "Would it have been alright with you if it said 'Jews in Favor of Genocide?'" the police reportedly "manhandled him even more fiercely." According to Iris Hefets, herself arrested for holding a similar sign in 2023, it appears that Jews have been specifically targeted for arrest because they "get in the way of the narrative."

One does not need to be a historian to recognize what is unsettling about German repression of Jews protesting genocide. While a court has since found the raid on the event unlawful, a climate of widespread censorship and harassment endures. As all of it is carried out in the name of protecting Jews and the meaning of the Holocaust, one feels that the world, or at least its words, have turned upside down. The German state has staked redemption for the Shoah on unquestionable support for Israel even as the far-right party Alternative for Deutschland, with an alarming record of antisemitism and Holocaust denial, increases its share of power in the Bundestag. Jews being arrested for insufficient loyalty to a Jewish state stands as a strange emblem of an absurdist present and a menacing echo of a fast-encroaching past.

It is this sense of inversion that historian Mark Mazower's new book, *On Antisemitism: A Word in History*, seeks to chronicle and explain. Opening with Victor Klemperer's account of the way language became "an instrument of power" under the Third Reich, Mazower suggests we are witnessing a similar kind of transformation today: a nationalist and imperialist right in Israel, Europe, and the United States—abetted by timid or overtly complicit liberals—changing the meaning of words not to capture a new reality but to transform it in the service of holding onto and furthering their power. The term "antisemitism," coined by a far right eager to couch its own Judeophobia in the modern language of scientific racism and later used as a term of condemnation to name that deadly form of bigotry, is now widely associated with hostility to the state of Israel, especially from Arab and Islamic quarters. How did a word originally intended to justify the exercise of state power over a long-persecuted Jewish minority come to serve as a tool for justifying the power of the Jewish state to persecute vulnerable and stateless Palestinians? That is the story Mazower wants to tell: the way the word tracks the history of state power as much as the history of Jews themselves.

It is a necessary intervention, deflating the specter of antisemitism that has long been deployed to justify attacks on universities, free speech, and Palestine itself, more intensely than ever in recent years. It is also a welcome rejoinder to books that have helped to give this panic moral and intellectual legitimacy, among them Bari Weiss's *How to Fight Anti-Semitism* (2019) and Holocaust scholar Deborah Lipstadt's *Antisemitism: Here and Now* (2019). Both effectively accuse the Palestine solidarity movement of working to eliminate the Jews from positions of prominence in universities and government, or worse. Given such attempts to whip the public into believing that new tracks are being laid for a twenty-first-century Auschwitz, this time by the left, Mazower seeks to force the term back into the more orderly confines of history. Antisemitism marked a particular moment in European history, he argues—a moment that was neither inevitable nor is likely to return.

There is something very satisfying in applying a historical strait-jacket to the paranoid style of American Zionist politics. One gets the sense that were cooler minds to prevail, perhaps much-needed clarity could be returned both to the word and to the larger discourse around anti-Jewish politics. Whether this approach is sufficient to place the sorcerer's brooms back in the closet, however, is less clear. Neither Jewish Zionists nor actual Judeophobes, it seems, are content to leave the gravestones at Babi Yar unmolested. In an era of neofascism, marked by both ethnonationalist genocide against Palestinians and the muscular reassertion of far-right racisms, it is possible that history may be accelerating faster than the clear delineations of linear analysis will allow.

TO BE SURE, evidence of a transformation in the meaning of "antisemitism" is everywhere one looks. Mazower devotes significant attention to the career of the "working definition" developed in 2004 by the International Holocaust Remembrance Alliance (IHRA), an intergovernmental organization founded in Stockholm and now headquartered in Berlin.

Antisemitism, the working definition states, "is a certain perception of Jews, which may be expressed as hatred toward Jews. Rhetorical and physical manifestations of antisemitism are directed toward Jewish or non-Jewish individuals and/or their property, toward Jewish community institutions and religious facilities." As Mazower rightly notes, this "says less and does so less clearly" than the definition given in the Oxford English Dictionary. The controversy concerns the IHRA's "contemporary examples" of antisemitism, which are alleged to include "claiming that the existence of a State of Israel is a racist endeavor," "drawing comparisons of contemporary Israeli policy to that of the Nazis," and applying "double standards" to Israel "by requiring of it a behavior not expected or demanded of any other democratic nation."

While the definition was originally intended as a tool for monitoring and research, the United States, Canada, and all but one member state of the European Union have made it legally binding. In 2019 the Trump administration issued an executive order requiring the federal government to abide by the definition and its examples for "robust enforcement of Title VI" of the Civil Rights Act. Joe Biden never rescinded the order, and subsequently several U.S. states passed laws incorporating the definition as well. The definition, Jared Kushner explained at the time, "makes clear what our administration has stated publicly and on the record: Anti-Zionism is anti-Semitism." While it is ambiguous what the definition's drafters hoped it would accomplish, Kushner's formula is a common refrain among those who endorse it.

There is thus a particular irony in the claim that Israel ought not be singled out for criticism: no other country besides Israel enjoys such protections in law or custom in these nations. Accusations of Slavophobia are never treated as civil or criminal transgressions, nor would alleging the settler origins of the Russian state or likening Putin to Hitler be deemed racist, any more than charges of Sinophobia are for questioning Han Chinese dominance over other ethnic minorities in the Republic of China. The consequences of adopting the IHRA definition have been severe, compounding existing legal instruments of repression such as anti-terrorism and anti-boycotting laws and supercharging attacks by pro-Israel or antisemitism watchdog groups, many of them backed by right-wing billionaires.

Antisemitism's "smokescreen" quality exposes, perhaps more clearly than ever before, that it has never really been about the Jews.

What makes this suppression of speech particularly perverse is that it is being pursued, both culturally and legally, in the name of fighting discrimination. In the words of a recent U.S. federal court ruling, antisemitism has been used as a "smokescreen." The disorienting result is what might be called *civil rights fascism*, with far-right GOP politicians like Elise Stefanik and billionaire financiers like Bill Ackman leading the charge, claiming student protesters are calling for the mass extermination of Jews. Public pressure campaigns inspired by their accusations have led to the resignation of Ivy League presidents and fueled lawsuits and federal complaints against pro-Palestine demonstrations and encampments. Challenges to academic freedom have weaponized Title VI lawsuits alleging discrimination or hostile environments against Jews and Israelis. Even where cases aren't legally successful, they change behavior, prompting risk-averse university administrators to suppress any speech they find liable to prompt lawsuits. The ultimate target isn't speech codes at elite U.S. colleges but the entire liberal legal framework around race, religion, and the law.

In one of the most remarkable of these cases, *Frankel v. Regents of the University of California*, a federal court found in favor of Jewish students who claimed that a UCLA student encampment, where protesters (including Jews) were violently attacked and ultimately forcibly cleared, violated their religious freedom when it limited entrance to anti-Zionist students. The ruling extends a long history of right-wing backlash politics that first emerged in response to the civil rights movement. In the highest-profile such case, again involving the University of California, a white plaintiff rejected from medical school, Allan Bakke, claimed that the school's affirmative action program discriminated against white people. The Anti-Defamation League (ADL) filed an amicus brief supporting Bakke, just as it now endorses the right-wing narrative that universities are "failing to fight antisemitism." When the Supreme Court ruled in *Bakke* only against racial quotas—rather than all forms of race-conscious affirmative action—the ADL's general counsel, Arnold Forster, expressed disappointment the justices had not gone all the way.

Using Title VI to crush Palestine solidarity protests, threaten and extort universities, and ban student organizations thus must be seen as part of a wider, much longer campaign against racial diversity programs and indeed the whole legacy of the civil rights era writ large. In Indiana, these attacks were revealingly combined in two laws passed in close succession by the legislature, one designed to "promote intellectual diversity" in light of Republican distrust of universities and the other to "make sure that Jewish students feel safe and welcome." Though the latter was vetoed by the governor, both framed their objective as protecting putatively white students against a woke mob of anticolonial students of color. In the Heritage Foundation's words, "Jewish students having to barricade themselves in a college . . . has opened people's eyes to the threat woke ideology represents to civilization." Anti-DEI crusades and anti-"antisemitism" are here one and the same.

MAZOWER RESPONDS to these alarming developments with his own definition of antisemitism. "The invention of the concept of antisemitism," he argues, "was part of the birth of the modern." In particular, it was "a reaction against modernity itself." Mazower stresses a rupture from the past when the term was introduced in 1879 by journalist

Wilhelm Marr's League of Antisemites and subsequently absorbed into the heady political contestation of post-unification Germany.

In this schema, "antisemitism" derives from the historical legacy of anti-Jewish bigotry or Judeophobia, which have their roots in millennia of Christian othering, but it is not synonymous with them. As Freud pointed out, Jewish continuity is a reminder of Christianity's inability to shake off its ancient traces; Jews remain a kind of stain in the fabric of historical cleansing promised by the new religion. In Mazower's telling, antisemitism instead names a certain kind of "politically organized" movement. Modern nation-states are born out of contradictory claims: universal citizenship on the one hand, the organic unification of a culturally and racially distinctive people on the other. The contradiction is both enhanced and exposed by a variety of forces, from the construction of a common market for global capitalism to military backing for private overseas imperial conquest. If the modern state is a universal form of belonging, it is also a committee, as Lenin famously said, for the organized bourgeoisie: it can't be, and yet must be, both.

According to Mazower, antisemitism, properly understood, emerged precisely from these contradictions, portraying "the Jews as singlehandedly responsible for pretty much every grievance contemporary life presented and did so using the preeminently modern vehicles of the popular press and party politics." Antisemitism is thus a particular kind of movement—an organized intervention into particular political crises—that seeks to rid the modern state of its internal other, exemplified by the figure of the unassimilable Jew who threatens the organic unity of the new polity. For Mazower, France's Dreyfus Affair clearly marks the difference between ancient Jew-hatred and modern antisemitism. In 1894 Alfred Dreyfus, an artillery captain in the French army of Jewish descent, was accused of treason by his superiors. The intelligentsia of the nascent left eventually came to his defense, sparking weeks of pogroms, violence, and street battles and entrenching the perception that antisemitism was the political vehicle for reactionary nationalism against an emergent socialism in a modern world seen as dislocating and oppressive.

Cutting against the grain of depictions of antisemitism as eternal and unchanging, Mazower describes the wave of anti-Jewish terror that seized fin-de-siècle Europe, from the Kishinev Pogrom to the *Protocols of the Elders of Zion*, as a short-lived, if "shocking," spasm of violence. Mazower uses the word again and again to describe attacks, beatings, murders, emphasizing their apparently surprising and arbitrary nature; the only people not surprised, in this account, are the Zionists, who thought "the hatred Jews faced from those around them was to be expected." Indeed, "had the First World War never been fought at all," Mazower imagines, the *soi-disant* antisemites might well have faded into history, much like royalists and speakers of Old Church Slavonic. It is an unusually large counterfactual to encounter in the work of a historian. "Where civil rights had been won," he writes of Europe in 1914, "they had not been rolled back." Until, of course, they were. With the vast industrial slaughter, marauding armies, and hypernationalism of the Great War, pogroms returned with a vengeance, killing Jews not in the hundreds but the thousands, even tens of thousands—the subsequent crises giving rise to fascism, and in particular to the Nazi Party.

Through the attacks of today's far right, anti-DEI crusades and anti-"antisemitism" have become one and the same.

Mazower's focus on the twists and turns, ups and downs of the antisemitic "movement" seems intended to dramatize how the Holocaust, or even antisemitism itself, was neither inevitable nor predicable. It "cannot be emphasized enough," he writes, how much the Nazis changed everything, "suddenly" placing Jews at the center of politics and then of world history with their attacks on "Jewish power" and specter of "Jewish war." Fascism thus appears to Mazower as rupture and discontinuity, throwing history off its steady progressive course. The implication is that but for the Nazis, antisemitism as a "world power" would not exist. Perhaps the Jews themselves, seen as a people whose lives and deaths have been the subject of empires and grand theory, would not have "mattered very much from the perspective of world history," indeed might have remained a "small, venerable sect bypassed by power, not unlike the Parsis or the Jains." Though in practical terms the Nazis succeeded in making Europe "Judenfrei," at least west of Moscow, their demise dealt a major blow to the strange obsession with Jews and Jewishness. "Anti-Jewish prejudices survived," Mazower concedes, "but antisemitism itself as a political movement was largely discredited in the region that had given birth to it." It would endure, he argues, in the Soviet Union. But starting in the early 1970s, emigration to Israel became possible in larger numbers and then exploded with the fall of the USSR and in the ensuing decades. For Mazower, "a major chapter in the history of antisemitism closed" with this last flight of Russian Jews.

The end of history, in this narrative, thus also marks the end of Jewish otherness. As Mazower notes, the centers of Jewish gravity have moved from Europe to the United States and Israel. In the latter, Jews became a demographic majority for the first time in the modern world, while in the former they found a society in which they could thrive, owing to what Mazower calls a "modern conception of all-inclusive citizenship." These are strange words to read in a moment of resurgent anti-immigrant terror, hardly an isolated or marginal phenomenon in U.S. history. Though Mazower notes that some French commentators saw a new Dreyfus Affair in the trial of Julius and Ethel Rosenberg on charges of espionage in the early 1950s, he downplays the event's significance with the dubious alibi that most of the prominent American Jewish institutions "did not share the widespread suspicion of the internationalist left that the case was a product of antisemitic Cold War hysteria."

In this telling, antisemitism barely registers in the American march to equality and inclusion. By the early 1970s, American Jews were living in a golden age of acceptance, prosperity, and security, unparalleled in history. It is true that the late 1960s witnessed a sharp decline in antisemitic attitudes and the end of the last antisemitic housing, educational, and immigration restrictions. Mazower says the change "defies simple explanation," but really it was part of a wider turn against racism and many other forms of bigotry following the peak of the civil rights movement and the rise of the New Left, which also secured progressive ideas of academic freedom and political expression.

Yet American Jewish institutions—including its ostensible civil rights organizations such as the ADL and American Jewish Committee (AJC)—did not welcome these developments as much as they might have. Rather than see the New Left and Black freedom struggles as part of a more liberal, multicultural America, they perceived these movements as an existential threat to Israel. In one of many epochal changes in the American Jewish world, the U.S. embrace of Israel as a Cold War ally against the Soviet-backed Arab states, especially after the Six-Day War in 1967, led to a dramatic institutional realignment from the lukewarm "non-Zionism" of the immediate postwar era to the muscular Zionism that still prevails—reframing Israel as the primary, even sole concern of American Jews. One consequence, Mazower points out, is that Palestinians ceased to be seen as displaced people seeking national liberation and instead came to be portrayed as antisemites: where they had once been a *national* enemy of an expanding Israeli state, they were now a *bigoted* enemy of a still-vulnerable global Jewish people. Meanwhile, leftist organizations went from being categorized as subversives to purveyors of racist and illiberal hate.

This "new antisemitism" thesis was crystallized in a 1974 book by that name authored by ADL leaders Benjamin Epstein and Arnold Forster—the latter the general counsel who would go on to file an amicus brief on behalf of Allan Bakke. What gave the thesis force was that it attracted the notice of neoconservatives and Orientalists in the State Department and the Pentagon. Scholars such as Bernard Lewis and Samuel Huntington, along with Defense Department figures such as Donald Rumsfeld, were eager to cast Middle Eastern rivals and the Soviet Union as bastions of racism and to further discredit an already waning anti-imperialist left with charges of antisemitism. Perhaps the most absurd early episode of this alliance occurred during the Reagan administration, when the State Department called the pro-Palestinian Nicaraguan Sandinista government antisemitic in an attempt to persuade American liberals that the leftist revolutionary state was threatening religious and ethnic minorities in the country. Tellingly, the one Jewish American to be assassinated in Nicaragua was an American socialist, Ben Linder, who traveled to Nicaragua to help rural communities establish electrical power. He was murdered by the Contras in 1987. His death, needless to say, was not investigated by the Reagan administration as an act of antisemitism, or for that matter even a crime.

But the new antisemitism thesis didn't really kick into high gear, either in the United States or European Union, until after September 11. The Global War on Terrorism launched in its wake relied both on the liberal, democratic rhetoric of "freedoms" as well as on Huntington's "clash of civilizations"—in particular, between a revanchist Muslim world mired

in social pathology and a Western liberal world of enlightenment rationality and consumer plenty. A "new cadre of antisemitism watchdogs"
flourished, Mazower notes, as nonprofits and Jewish institutions were
absorbed into new governance structures such as the Organization for
Security and Co-Operation in Europe and the U.S. State Department's
Office of the Special Envoy to Monitor and Combat Antisemitism.
Accusations of antisemitism became a tool for projecting American and
European imperial power in the name of defeating illiberal Muslim states
and loosely organized terror networks, just as it serves today as a tool
for exercising state control over universities in the name of protecting
Jewish students. The specter of the "Islamofascist," so prominent after
9/11, combined the historic defeat of Nazi Germany with a new enemy of
the American imperium, the figural Jew again needing to be saved—this
time in the form of the state of Israel. If civil rights fascism is the logic of
the new anti-antisemitism in the United States, human rights imperialism is this logic applied abroad.

Neither Jewish Zionists nor actual Judeophobes, it seems, are content to leave the gravestones at Babi Yar unmolested.

The effect of all this has been to cement the changing meaning of
"antisemitism." By 2016, the IHRA had formally adopted its working
definition and examples. Monitoring the new antisemitism has become
a matter of surveillance, discipline, and law, so much so that paying lip
service to combatting antisemitism is all that is needed—from Trump to
Viktor Orbán to Boris Johnson—to be welcomed into the polite society
of Western nations. This has led scholars such as Enzo Traverso to claim
that the structures of exclusion and marginalization once associated
with the term have been wholly subsumed by Islamophobia. Others,
such as Barry Trachtenberg, have concluded "antisemitism" is no longer a useful term at all and should be replaced by "anti-Jewish hatred."
Mazower ends by returning to Klemperer, who wrote of the process
by which "a currently highly fashionable expression, one apparently
never destined to be expunged, suddenly goes silent [and] disappears
with the context that gave birth to it." A long historical cycle, with the
Holocaust and the fight against fascism at its center, is over, Mazower

implies, and "antisemitism" might soon become just such a "fossil" as Klemperer imagined.

ALL THIS GOES a long way to substantiating what the likes of Weiss and Lipstadt get wrong. At the same time Mazower's paeans to American liberal democracy ring hollow in the present moment. In hindsight, the "golden age" of Jewish assimilation he describes—part of the broader legacy of the civil rights era and the New Left the book says little about— looks to have been only a brief thaw in the longer arc of America's post– Civil War attack on Reconstruction, racial equality, and the left.

The book oddly conveys little of American antisemitism in particular, from Civil War forced removals to the Immigration Act of 1924 (which created the U.S. Border Patrol, prevented the vast majority of Jews from fleeing Nazi Germany, and barred immigration from Asia entirely). Perhaps the most familiar example of state-sponsored antisemitism, the midcentury Red Scare, goes by in a single sentence. Its central conceit— that a cabal of secretive communists was plotting to undermine America from within, in league with the Soviet Union—was only a slightly softer version of the Nazi's own "Judeo-Bolshevik threat." The greatest attack on Jews since the Holocaust took place not October 7 but in the late 1970s and early 1980s when the Argentine Junta, backed by the United States and armed with weapons from Israel, killed at least 1,296 and possibly as many as 3,000 Jews in its own Red Scare. Mazower's narrative effectively relegates all this to a distant past.

All signs rather suggest that history is not quite over. While both liberals and conservatives target Palestine solidarity activists in the name of anti-antisemitism, the Republican Party has a vocal and growing antisemitic base. In Mazower's own terms, this is anti-Jewish sentiment not only as ancient prejudice but as organized political movement—antisemitism, that is, in the modern sense. Trump's Jew-baiting political ads and invocations of Soros conspiracy theories cannot be dismissed as shocking but isolated phenomena, paroxysms of a mad king. Not only are they voiced by the most powerful head of the most powerful state in the world; they represent a crucial plank of the far-right worldview.

At a recent conference hosted by Turning Point USA (TPUSA)—the unofficial youth wing of the GOP—J. D. Vance contrasted his party of "free thinkers" to "a bunch of drones who take their orders from George Soros." That was shortly after Steve Bannon said, to mass applause, that kippah-clad Ben Shapiro—himself a speaker at the conference—"is like a cancer, and that cancer spreads." Last year, at another TPUSA event, a student pressed Vance about the unreasonableness of conservative support for Israel, concluding: "Not only does their religion not agree with ours, but [it] also openly supports the prosecution of ours."

The vice president, of course, has worked for years to renovate a white nativism obsessed with heritage and ancestry; at a revealing moment in a book event with Charles Murray after the release of Vance's memoir in 2016, the two shared a laugh about what Murray called their "pretty clean Scots-Irish blood." When news broke last year about a group chat of Young Republican leaders joking about Hitler and gas chambers, Vance made a point of refusing to condemn it. Meanwhile, popular podcasters such as Candace Owens and Nick Fuentes broadcast a toxic mix of far-right and Christian antisemitism to their millions of followers. When the center-right political establishment uniformly and brutally represses criticism of Israel, it is not hard to understand why some welcome the apparently bold truth-telling of Owens, Fuentes, and Tucker Carlson. The reality, however, is that they are mobilizing popular outrage at Israel to normalize an antisemitic, Christian nationalist view of the world. That the far right should hope to capitalize on this moment should come as no surprise. A long line of Jewish writers and intellectuals, from Hannah Arendt to Maxime Rodinson, Judah Magnes, and Isaac Deutscher, have warned that Israel's crimes, including the violence and displacement at its creation, would fuel antisemitic reaction.

Then there is the odd confluence between attacks on "woke" universities and pro-Palestine activists, captured succinctly in a headline from the Heritage Foundation: "How Cultural Marxism Threatens the United States—and How Americans Can Fight It." As Noah Berlatsky has noted in *Jewish Currents*, the trope of "cultural Marxism" began as the Nazi's "cultural Bolshevism" and has since been picked up by Holocaust denier William Lind, mass shooter Anders Breivik, and antisemitic theorist Kevin MacDonald to decry the Jewishness of the Frankfurt School and the supposed Jewish origins of identity politics, cultural studies, feminism, and other poisons emanating from the academy. The second half of the headline opposes the "Marxists" to the "Americans," implying, of course, that such ideas are not only radical and subversive but, like the rootless, cosmopolitan Jews who authored them, inherently foreign, intrinsically other. We thus have an even odder phenomenon than Mazower describes—Jews are said to be under assault, and defending them means peddling an antisemitic conspiracy theory coined and spread by neo-Nazis. One of the organizations most clearly targeted by Heritage's Project 2025 is Jewish Voice for Peace, among the largest Jewish civic organizations in this country, with tens of thousands of members and hundreds of thousands of supporters.

In our era of neofascism, history may be accelerating faster than clear delineations will allow.

Far from antisemitism being over, then, we are witnessing its mutation into a new and contradictory form, one that dispenses with Jews even as it relies on the old specter of Jewishness for its potency. As Heritage's strange fusion of antisemitism with anti-antisemitism makes plain, "protecting Jews" has become yet another way to advance a blood-and-soil nationalism for which the mythic and ephemeral figure of the Judeo-Bolshevik, in the guise of Soros or the shadowy cultural Marxist, is still an enemy. As this specter did for the Nazis, it permits a wide class of targets, in this case not only or even most Jews but migrants, socialists real and imagined, sexual and gender minorities, protesters of all stripes—anyone perceived and deemed a threat to the völkisch order. As Shane Burley and Ben Lorber make clear in their guidebook on fighting antisemitism, *Safety Through Solidarity* (2024), racism is relational, not nominal or definitional: how the right understands the migrant and Marxist is bound up in how they understand the figural Jew, the African American, the whole of multicultural and egalitarian America.

Stuart Hall observed that one of the lasting myths of historicism—we might say of liberalism too—is the "smooth march of a historical evolutionism." ("Surely if liberalism has a single desperate weakness," even the liberal Lionel Trilling once noted, "it is an inadequacy of imagination: liberalism is always being surprised.") Both Mazower, in this historicizing book, and those he rightly criticizes believe in an orderly march of some kind: for Mazower antisemitism is finished, and the term has been nearly evacuated of meaning; for Zionists and other wielders of state power, antisemitism endures, however transformed into anti-Zionism, which implies their own righteousness does as well. The two positions are mirror images, both narratives of hoped-for continuity. Neither can imagine where the unhoped-for continuities may lie.

The irony of contemporary antisemitism is that its increasingly contradictory, "smokescreen" quality exposes, perhaps more clearly than ever before, that antisemitism has never really been about the Jews: it has always been a discourse, the object of which is history and power itself. While Jews will remain its victims—in stochastic hate crimes, university firings, arrests by German and American police—Palestine and Palestinians are now its principal targets, along with U.S. civil society itself. Max Horkheimer and Theodor Adorno got it right already in 1947: "the victims are interchangeable." If we are puzzled by this contradiction, it is only because "the anti-Semitic psychology has largely been replaced by mere acceptance of the whole fascist ticket." **BR**

MAKING THE DEPORTATION MACHINE
Marie Gottschalk

The Migrant's Jail: An American History of Mass Incarceration
Brianna Nofil
Princeton University Press, $32

The Highest Law in the Land: How the Unchecked Power of Sheriffs
Threatens Democracy
Jessica Pishko
Dutton/Penguin Random House, $32

The Minneapolis Reckoning: Race, Violence, and the Politics of Policing
in America
Michelle S. Phelps
Princeton University Press, $29.95

Copaganda: How Police and the Media Manipulate Our News
Alec Karakatsanis
New Press, $31.99

IN THE RECENT FILM *One Battle After Another*, the line between immigration enforcement and law enforcement has vanished in the United States. The constitutional and human rights of citizens and noncitizens alike are evaporating as brutal immigration crackdowns fuel political repression and ignite blasts of violence. The odious Colonel Stephen J. Lockjaw—chillingly played by Sean Penn, with an uncanny resemblance to recently reassigned U.S. Border Patrol commander Gregory Bovino—slithers between immigration authorities, local police, the armed forces, and white supremacist militias. He is finally punished not by state authorities acting under the force of law but rather by his white supremacist frenemies, who execute him because he has become a political liability.

Whatever one makes of the politics of the film, it is hard not to be struck by its resonances with the present. Donald Trump's militant mass deportation operation can only be described in terms the administration reserves for protesters: it is a campaign of terror, backed by the full force and effect of the federal government. In jurisdictions across the country, masked immigration authorities, troops, local police, and sheriffs' departments are working in lockstep to carry out this mission. The lives claimed include not only Renee Good and Alex Pretti in Minneapolis but also a Cuban man, Geraldo Lunas Campos, whose death under Immigration and Customs Enforcement (ICE) detention at Camp East Montana in Texas was ruled a homicide in January, as well as at least thirty-two others who have died in conditions deplored by human rights groups as inhumane, illegal, and barbaric. All the while, some state and local authorities and especially the public are pushing back against the feds or preparing to resist the onslaught when their time comes.

How did we get here? Blaming Trump or Stephen Miller, his deputy chief of staff for homeland security, only gets us so far. For anyone seeking to stem state violence and mitigate the brutalities and injustices of the existing order, understanding how the criminal legal system and immigration enforcement have been braided together is essential. So is understanding the central but often overlooked role of sheriffs' departments and the political economy of rural areas as bulwarks of the carceral and deportation state. Several recent books paint a stark portrait of the uniquely expansive regime of U.S. policing and punishment, revealing what conventional wisdom gets wrong about its origins and scale and clarifying the obstacles to changing it.

THERE IS PERHAPS no better place to start in tracing the roots of this moment than *The Migrant's Jail*, historian Brianna Nofil's magisterial study of the mutual development of U.S. penal and immigration policy over more than a century. The political and institutional pillars of the system as we know it today were not put in place relatively recently, Nofil shows. On the contrary, they emerged over decades through bipartisan consensus and complex interactions between federal, state, and local authorities.

The story begins in the late 1800s, by which time U.S. courts had reached a consensus that local governments were not free to forge or execute their own immigration policies. Whether and how the federal government might coerce or cajole localities to carry out federal immigration policies remained unsettled, however. The pitched battles today between the Trump administration and certain states and municipalities over sanctuary status, detention facilities, and cooperation with ICE are being fought on this still indeterminate terrain. But such antagonism is more the historical exception than the rule, Nofil demonstrates. Over the long run, the dominant pattern has been mutually beneficial cooperation between the federal government, states, counties, and cities.

The pillars of the system were not put in place recently. They emerged over decades through bipartisan consensus.

Indeed, county jails have always been "foundational to the project of federal immigration law enforcement," Nofil explains, yet "they have operated with a staggering absence of oversight or public awareness." Numbering nearly 3,000 for more than a century now, these facilities have functioned as a win-win in the eyes of government officials. On the one hand, they have allowed policy set in Washington to expand its reach far beyond ports and borders. On the other hand, federal contracts have served as cash cows for local communities, enabling them to expand jail space, cushion budgets, reduce taxes, and create slush funds for local officials. Working with federal authorities has thus long empowered cities and counties to bankroll carceral expansion without having to seek the tax dollars or the approval of voters. Last summer, the sheriff who oversees Butler County Jail in Ohio put it plainly: the federal government "depends on sheriffs and county jails to have bed space," and his recently renewed ICE contract helps "pay the bills."

In moving detail, Nofil brings to life the voices of hungry, sick, sweltering, and shivering migrants caught up in the immigration system through the decades, many of whom were driven to suicide or its brink while languishing in detention. One common thread she finds in their stories is the "agonizing uncertainty" of being subject to the whims of state power. Ellen Knauff, a German woman detained in 1948 while trying to enter the country with her American husband, was held for more than a year at Ellis Island; detainees are "shut away from the outside world long enough," she later observed in a memoir, that "most of them will stop caring about what happens in the world as well as to themselves." Knauff's habeas petition went to the Supreme Court, whose ruling helped enshrine the so-called "entry fiction" and plenary power doctrines, depriving entering aliens of due process rights and exempting deportation orders from judicial review in most cases. Nor have justifications for treatment like the kind Knauff faced been solely legalistic. Politicians and policymakers have long portrayed deplorable detention conditions as vital means for deterring immigration or encouraging self-deportation, Nofil shows. Trump's cruel spectacle of "Alligator Alcatraz"—and for that matter, Obama's quieter determination to detain families in prison-like conditions—thus cannot be seen as exceptional.

Perhaps the most striking antecedent of today's mass deportation campaign is "Operation Wetback," a federal spectacle launched by the Eisenhower administration in 1953 that remains largely unknown to the public, despite Trump's many oblique references to it since his first presidential campaign. Over the span of two years, immigration authorities apprehended and removed more than 800,000 Mexican migrants "from work camps, bars, and the streets of American communities, as fawning media coverage celebrated the heroics of the Border Patrol's war on Mexicans," Nofil notes. The operation simultaneously entrenched the depiction of migrants as criminals and as an existential, racialized threat. At the time, Immigration and Naturalization Service (INS) Commissioner Joseph Swing called migration from Mexico "an actual invasion of the United States," a message that helped to neutralize claims that deplorable immigration policy was undermining the image of the United States as a beacon of human rights in the Cold War. By the 1970s, many local police and sheriffs' departments had embraced immigration enforcement as central to crime-fighting. Between 1968 and 1978, the number of migrants turned over to the INS exploded about twelvefold to 120,000 annually thanks to the growing use of "detainer" requests from federal authorities.

This "rebranding" of immigration enforcement as law enforcement only further accelerated the following decade, Nofil shows. Under Attorney General Edwin Meese, Ronald Reagan's Department of Justice explicitly identified the INS as "a criminal justice agency." Meanwhile, beginning in the 1980s, Congress enacted several land-mark measures fostering collaboration between the INS and local law enforcement, lengthening the list of deportable offenses and bolstering the government's capacity to detain citizens and noncitizens alike. The Immigration Reform and Control Act of 1986 provided a pathway for millions of unauthorized migrants to legalize their status, but this so-called amnesty legislation also mandated that deportation be carried out "as expeditiously as possible" after someone is found guilty of a deportable offense. To facilitate that, the INS established the Alien Criminal Apprehension Program to share information with local law enforcement, further entrenching their relationship.

And then there were the high-profile crime bills, first under Reagan and then under Bill Clinton, which included provisions for getting tough on noncitizens that received little public attention at the time but wound up fueling the deportation machine. In addition to their infamously discriminatory penalties for possession of crack cocaine, the Anti-Drug Abuse Acts of 1986 and 1988 stipulated that noncitizens convicted of an "aggravated felony," including "nearly all drug offenses," were subject to deportation. A decade later, a pair of laws signed by Clinton—the Antiterrorism and Effective Death Penalty Act and the Illegal Immigration Reform and Immigrant Responsibility Act (IIRIRA)—enlarged the pool of aggravated felonies, expanded the list of deportable offenses to include certain misdemeanors, and ren-dered noncitizens subject to deportation for offenses adjudicated years or even decades earlier. Furthermore, the IIRIRA called for mandatory detention for a broad set of immigration violations.

As with all laws, the reach and impact of these measures depended on political will and institutional capacity. The federal government accrued more of both by offering funding and other incentives for local and state authorities to expand the carceral state. The Reagan admin-istration initiated the Cooperative Agreement Program, which granted local governments hundreds of millions of dollars for jail construction in exchange for guarantees that the federal government could use the space, including to detain migrants. The most sweeping of Clinton's crime bills, the Violent Crime Control and Law Enforcement Act of 1994, institutionalized federal reimbursement for the cost of local detainment through the State Criminal Alien Assistance Program, which has always been rife with fraud and abuse. Programs established in the late 2000s gave both police and correctional authorities quick access to federal biometric databases to check the immigration status not only of people already held in custody but also those stopped for questioning or a minor traffic violation—tools that made it easier both to deport migrants and to make a dollar off doing so.

All the while, the criminal legal system and the immigration enforcement system were knitted ever closer together. Especially significant has been the IIRIRA's 287(g) program permitting federal immigration authorities to deputize police officers and sheriffs to carry out key functions, including interrogating and arresting people suspected of violating immigration law. Testifying to Congress in 2005, an ICE official told lawmakers the program would target criminals, not the "landscaping type of individuals." But around half of arrests under the program begin with routine traffic stops. By recruiting localities to be "the foot soldiers of immigration law enforcement" through these and other measures, the federal government "enabled a diffusion of political consequences and further obscured who held power over immigration," Nofil writes. The wide discretionary power granted to local law enforcement fostered "a form of racialized social control."

BY THE EARLY twenty-first century, the United States was thus already in the throes of what some have called a "crimmigration" or "immcarceration" crisis hiding in plain sight. When ICE was created in 2003—part of the new Department of Homeland Security, established in the wake of the September 11 attacks—it replaced the INS and effectively became the largest law enforcement agency in the country. Prosecutions for immigration-related offenses came to comprise more than half of the federal prosecutorial caseload—up from about 10 to 20 percent during the preceding two decades and far surpassing prosecutions for drug, white-collar, and other offenses.

Yet this "crimmigration" crisis has rarely figured in growing attention to the origins and ills of "mass incarceration." Michelle Alexander's book *The New Jim Crow* (2010) helped thrust the latter phrase into popular consciousness, but it made only passing reference to immigration. Four years later, the National Academy of Sciences (NAS) released a landmark study on mass incarceration's causes and consequences. The United States had become the world's warden, the report stressed, locking up more of its people than nearly any other country. But the NAS panel, which I served on, had surprisingly little to say about the role of immigration policy in fueling the carceral state—even as U.S. jails and prisons were detaining record numbers of people on immigration-related charges and migrant advocates were reviling Obama as the "deporter-in-chief." The government-reported average daily number of ICE detainees has skyrocketed from around 21,000 in 2003 to 73,000 as of this writing in early 2026—the highest on record. But these figures are surely gross undercounts: they do not include people on holds or detainers in local jails and those held by the U.S. Marshals Service, Federal Bureau of Prisons, state detention in Florida and Texas, and secretive holding facilities in ICE offices.

To achieve this growth, the federal government has poured enormous amounts of money into expanding detention capacity of its own. Since ICE's creation, the agency's budget has increased nearly fivefold in inflation-adjusted dollars. Between fiscal years 2024 and 2025 alone it tripled to $28.7 billion—about five times the budget of the NYPD and three times that of the FBI—thanks to supplemental funding from the Big Beautiful Bill that Trump signed last July. Much of this additional spending is earmarked for recruiting thousands of new agents and expanding detention beds to at least 100,000 in order to facilitate the administration's goal of one million deportations annually. Nofil poignantly reminds us that each so-called detention bed represents "a life and a story, a set of circumstances that led a person to leave their homeland for an unknown life in the United States."

This expansion of federal capacity over the last two decades came with shifts in the "immigration federalism" at the heart of Nofil's narrative. Federal officials have long responded to reports of abusive treatment of migrants by scapegoating local authorities, portraying them as racist, uneducated enforcers. No doubt, some of them were, and are. But the attacks have also been part of a strategy: using publicity and lawsuits about abhorrent conditions in local jails to muster support for constructing supposedly humane alternatives under Washington's direct control. As Nofil illustrates in mournful detail, federal detention facilities have long been rife with abuses themselves.

In a much-needed corrective to accounts that associate mass incarceration primarily or solely with urban centers, Nofil shows that uproars over conditions at facilities close to metro areas prompted "the weaponization of remoteness." In the last two decades of the twentieth century, federal authorities began seeking out isolated communities for migrant detention, whether in existing jails or newly constructed federal and privately run facilities. Faced with unfavorable developments in one area—uprisings, hunger strikes, lawsuits, high-profile suicides, congressional investigations, growing political opposition, public scrutiny—the INS and now ICE have proven to be masters at disappearing noncitizens (and sometimes citizens) to parts of the country where the political and judicial landscape is more hospitable.

This "crimmigration" crisis has rarely figured in growing attention to the origins and ills of mass incarceration.

The result has been to build up the carceral heartland, especially in the South and Southwest—states like Louisiana, Florida, Texas, and Arizona. Well over 1,000 new jails, prisons, and detention centers have been constructed in the United States over the last four decades, disproportionately in rural and remote localities. Sociologist John Eason has documented how widely prisons were once stigmatized throughout the country, even in rural areas, but that changed beginning in the 1970s. With economies in freefall, rural communities wracked by deindustrialization and poverty started competing to become prison towns and hubs for immigration detention. New facilities were no longer seen as a "locally undesirable land use" akin to incinerators and dumps—in the wake of economic devastation and political abandonment, they promised salvation.

This transformation of the heartland cannot be understood solely in terms of white communities profiting off the caging of people of color. On the contrary, some rural areas with sizable Black and Latino populations welcomed new penal facilities; in many cases, the economic turnaround promised by expanding carceral capacity brought white, Black, and Latino residents together in areas with a history of racial conflict. Nor did all predominantly white communities go along. Nofil cites the example of Roswell, New Mexico, where a contractor failed in its 1983 bid to construct what would have been the first sizable private detention center in the country. One local observer presciently remarked, "Think of the consequences. . . . what civil and human rights could be violated without anyone even knowing it?" But on the whole, the expanding carceral state became an increasingly rural phenomenon.

Two decades ago, with rates of street crime falling and state and local governments facing enormous budgetary pressures, it appeared that the momentum for locking up so many people in the United States might be ebbing. Bipartisan talk of reform, even an air of optimism, came into vogue. And indeed, incarceration rates started to level off and then dip slightly, not least thanks to the growing strength of urban-based criminal justice reform movements that pushed for reduced penalties, alternatives to incarceration, and ending the war on drugs. But downward trends in aggregate rates don't tell the whole story: while prison admissions have plummeted for residents of big cities, admissions in many rural and smaller metro areas have continued to rise. In the mid-2000s, residents of rural, suburban, and urban areas had about an equal chance of being sent to prison; a decade later, people in small counties were about 50 percent more likely to end up in prison than people in larger urban areas. Since then rates have surged even further. And as economic and political conditions have changed, so have the demographics of the incarcerated. Interlocking systems of punishment, disadvantage, and violence have increasingly spread beyond the hyperincarceration of Black men.

In short, the so-called "era of criminal justice reform" has bypassed much of rural America. With social safety nets even more threadbare than those in urban areas, rural communities lack vital services and programs to keep people out of prison and jail. They also face acute shortages of prosecutors, judges, and public defenders, struggling to provide even basic legal services. But one thing that pockets of rural America do have is enormous carceral capacity and potential. The impact of federal detention contracts on local revenues can be substantial. Between 1980 and 1988, Nofil notes, the annual budget of the sheriff's office in Louisiana's Avoyelles Parish more than septupled to $5.5 million as the politically ambitious sheriff of the poor rural town constructed a sprawling migrant detention apparatus. By the end of the decade, his department employed more than 400 deputies—enough "to start an army," as one resident put it. After state lawmakers approved modest measures to reduce sentences in 2017, officials in another small town, Jackson Parish, faced a bind: With declining revenues, how could they cover jail construction bonds and avoid laying off guards? There and beyond, lucrative ICE contracts have proven the answer.

THE EXTRAORDINARY EXPANSION of the carceral and deportation apparatus has had far-reaching consequences, including helping to propel the radical rightward shift in U.S. politics. One way it has done so, journalist and lawyer Jessica Pishko shows in *The Highest Law in the Land*, is by bolstering the clout of powerful, shadowy, and unaccountable sheriffs with deep ties to the far right and white power movement. While the militarization of police departments—especially in major cities—has drawn ever more attention and criticism over the last decade, sheriffs continue to operate with relatively little scrutiny on the national stage. Pishko casts much-needed light on their unique role in the carceral state, the growing political power they wield, and the distinctive threat they pose to democracy.

The picture she paints begins with raw numbers. Employing about a quarter of the country's uniformed law enforcement officers, the roughly 3,000 sheriffs' departments spread throughout the United States have many of the same functions and duties as police departments and then some. Not only are sheriffs and their deputies the primary arresting officers in wide swaths of the country, especially rural areas; they also operate 85 percent of local jails, which hold about a third of the U.S. incarcerated population. Many departments are responsible for issuing permits and licenses for firearms as well as overseeing evictions. Many have exploited the expanding carceral state to great financial gain—including by brokering lucrative contracts to house citizens, noncitizens, and migrants, skimping on food and other necessities in penal operations, and taking kickbacks from telephone companies that charge incarcerated people exorbitant rates to make calls. And it's all profoundly racialized: some 90 percent of sheriffs, Pishko reports, are white men.

With economies in freefall, rural communities started competing to become prison towns and hubs for immigration detention.

Moreover, the system enjoys an unusual degree of autonomy and impunity within the U.S. political order. Unlike police chiefs and state troopers, sheriffs are elected officials who do not report to mayors, city councils, or governors. In much of the country, no one clearly has the power to arrest or remove them from office, even in grievous cases where they have been accused of serious crimes. Over half of all sheriffs' elections are uncontested, and incumbents virtually always win reelection; it is not uncommon for sheriffs to hold office for forty or even fifty years. One of the most infamous figures in contemporary anti-immigrant politics, Joe Arpaio, served as sheriff of Maricopa County in Arizona for almost a quarter-century before finally losing to a Democratic challenger in 2017. Styling himself as "America's Toughest Sheriff," Arpaio faced numerous misconduct charges and civil rights lawsuits over the course of his career and became a vocal supporter of Trump after leaving office. The president pardoned him in 2017 for contempt of federal court after a judge ordered Arpaio to stop detaining people solely on suspicion of being undocumented and the sheriff kept doing so, even bragging to PBS Newshour: "I'm still going to do what I'm doing."

Arpaio is hardly an isolated exception. Pishko illuminates the stakes and scale of sheriffs' power by chronicling the rise of the Constitutional Sheriffs and Peace Officers Association (CSPOA). Founded in 2011 by Richard Mack, another onetime sheriff in Arizona, the organization portrays sheriffs as bulwarks against tyranny, stewards of the Constitution, and the embodiment of public will. As such, CSPOA claims, sheriffs have the right and authority to resist laws and policies that violate the Constitution as they interpret it—from gun restrictions to mask mandates and abortion rights.

Although only a minority of sheriffs belong to Mack's organization, the group has played an outsize role in mainstreaming far-right ideas. Under Reagan, the main professional organization for sheriffs, the National Sheriffs' Association (NSA), supported modest gun control measures; now it is more or less totally aligned with the hardline stance of the National Rifle Association, which named Mack its officer of the year in 1994. Three-quarters of New Mexico's sheriffs identify their counties as "Second Amendment sanctuaries," Pishko notes—areas where state and federal gun control laws are not enforced. Though the NSA has disavowed Mack's claims in the past, "it has not made an official statement about the constitutional sheriff movement in over a decade," Pishko stresses. Sheriffs have also been key messengers in raising public doubts about the integrity of U.S. elections even as they trumpet their own elected status as a token of political legitimacy. They were central figures in the "Stop the Steal" campaign to overturn the results of the 2020 election, and they have been at the forefront of growing efforts to intimidate get-out-the-vote groups and interfere in election administration, asserting a dubious constitutional right to deputize private citizens to assist in allegations of voter fraud.

The legacy of the Jim Crow South thus in many ways endures. In still further echoes of that period, Pishko recounts chilling examples of sheriffs working hand-in-hand with right-wing militias, just as sheriffs in the South often allied with the Ku Klux Klan. Mack himself has been a board member of the Oath Keepers, a far-right extremist organization whose founder was convicted of seditious conspiracy for his role in the January 6 attacks on the U.S. Capitol. (Trump commuted his eighteen-year sentence last year.) During the national wave of protests following the murder of George Floyd by Minneapolis police officer Derek Chauvin in May 2020, armed militias throughout the country organized counterprotests with the explicit or tacit support of sheriffs. Pishko relates a particularly disturbing incident in which one department failed to intervene as militia members swarmed a group of Black Lives Matter activists marching in the small town of Minden, Nevada, in August that year. Officers stood aside while six hundred or more militia members and their supporters, many heavily armed, threatened, spat upon, and assaulted protesters; one man appeared to intentionally target demonstrators when he drove his pickup truck into them, striking two teenage girls.

In all this, *The Highest Law in the Land* masterfully excavates how sheriffs have fomented political violence, especially in areas far from the national spotlight. It also documents the gruesome and inhumane conditions endemic to local jails that sheriffs preside over. But there is even more that could be said to substantiate the antidemocratic threat posed by sheriffs' departments and local police alike—namely, through the quotidian violence of everyday law enforcement itself. U.S. rates of lethal use of force dwarf those in every other wealthy democracy, yet geographic disparities are not widely appreciated. Part of the reason is the "fetish of secrecy" that shrouds policing in the United States, as legal scholar Barry Friedman has put it. Reliable figures aren't collected and maintained by the government, and even data and records that do exist are hard to access. But according to the best available estimates, about three-quarters of police killings of civilians took place in rural and suburban areas last year, and sheriffs' departments are responsible for a disproportionate and growing share—more than a third as of year-end.

WHAT IS TO BE DONE? In *The Minneapolis Reckoning*, sociologist Michelle S. Phelps convincingly demonstrates that stemming police violence is highly dependent on grasping and navigating the nuances of local politics. She makes this case through a granular case study of efforts to reform the Minneapolis Police Department (MPD) between 2017 and 2023—the years leading up to and following Floyd's death and the mobilization of millions of protesters across the country calling for change. As the city once again reckons with explosive state violence and repression following the killing of unarmed civilians, Phelps's book provides tragically timely insight into the obstacles facing renewed calls to defund the police and rein in the carceral-deportation complex more broadly.

In the aftermath of Floyd's killing—and in the shadow of years, even decades, of activism to reform policing in the city—the Minneapolis City Council unanimously approved a ballot initiative aimed at amending the city's charter so as to replace a section on the MPD with new text calling for the creation of a Department of Community Safety and Violence Prevention. The key difference was that the language for the former required funding a minimum number of cops per capita, whereas the latter would permit but not require police officers. While the immediate practical significance of the change may have been vague, it hardly amounted in itself to defunding or abolishing the police, but many opponents and proponents of the measure characterized it as such. In the end, a legally prescribed commission for reviewing all proposed amendments originating with the city council voted to keep the proposal off the 2020 ballot. Thanks to a citizen-led initiative, the proposal did appear on the ballot a year later, but it was defeated in a highly contentious election in which Mayor Jacob Frey, who opposed the measure, was reelected.

For a variety of reasons, Phelps shows, the MPD and its allies succeeded in pitting concerns about police violence against concerns about community violence. The department was facing a legitimacy crisis as officers left in droves, morale sank, community ties were strained to the breaking point, and the Department of Justice opened an investigation into the city's long and troubling pattern of running roughshod over civil and constitutional rights. Meanwhile a steep spike in homicides beginning in 2020, fueled by the turbulent social disruption of COVID-19, divided potential allies for comprehensive reform. Medaria Arradondo, the department's first Black chief, told a youth task force in July 2021, "The biggest threat to public safety in our city, specifically the African American community" was not the police. "We have an epidemic right now of unequivocal gun violence, particularly in our African American communities, and that must stop." In the end, such opposition, in these conditions, helped law enforcement reclaim the mantle of public safety heroism. But although efforts to overhaul policing in Minneapolis ultimately failed, they loosened the MPD's "stranglehold on city politics— opening up more space for radical imagination," Phelps concludes.

In *Copaganda*, civil rights attorney Alec Karakatsanis further illuminates what the radical imagination is up against, mapping the "gulf between the image and the reality of the punishment bureaucracy" and the powerful institutions that "influence how we think about crime and safety." His principal targets aren't Fox News and the *New York Post*—brash champions of law enforcement—so much as legacy print and TV media (the *New York Times*, *Washington Post*, and NPR as much as MSNBC, CNN, and ABC News) and local news organizations (where they still exist). Under the guise of neutrality, he persuasively argues, these pillars of mainstream journalism produce stories, sometimes based on the work of criminologists at top universities and often in close collaboration with law enforcement agencies themselves, that effectively function as propaganda. The effect is to conceal the staggering scale of abuse in the system, manufacture consent for an ever-expanding carceral state, and inoculate police and the broader criminal legal system from comprehensive reform and democratic control.

Rejecting efforts to open a new detention center, one resident remarked, "Think of the consequences. . . . what civil and human rights could be violated without anyone even knowing it?"

Such "copaganda" can take many forms, Karakatsanis explains. It stokes public fears of crime by misrepresenting crime trends and minimizing or ignoring violence committed by law enforcement and prison guards. It covers street and violent crime in wild disproportion both to its actual frequency and to white-collar crime and corporate malfeasance. It promotes more police and prisons as solutions to crime panics even though a mountain of evidence undermines the idea that expanding the carceral apparatus enhances public safety. And it denigrates or marginalizes efforts to attack the root causes of crime, from greater investment in public education to affordable housing, a robust safety net, and universal health care.

In addition to the dissemination of copaganda through news media, Karakatsanis also documents the growing capacity of law enforcement to shape public opinion through their own booming public relations operations. While the *Chicago Tribune* was hemorrhaging jobs over the last decade, the PR arm of the Chicago Police Department mushroomed from six full-time employees in 2015 to fifty-five as of last year, Karakatsanis reports. All the while, police and law enforcement organizations have become increasingly sophisticated about managing their image—from ghostwriting op-eds and testing messages on focus groups to generously funding sympathetic academics, publishing slick PR videos on social media, and more.

For Karakatsanis, one of the most egregious effects of copaganda has been to misrepresent small-bore changes in police policy as transformative reforms of the system. In reality, he documents, many of the most widely discussed or even celebrated proposals, from body cameras to calls for greater training, not only do not rein in the policing apparatus but often help expand it. What's more, after the seemingly reasonable reform *du jour* fails to stem state violence or abuse of power, the public conversation in mainstream media and newsrooms moves on to another modest proposal, continuing to paint calls for more thoroughgoing change as unreasonable and dangerous radicalism. It is easier for academics, journalists, and other opinionmakers to get attention, Karakatsanis writes, "if they can propose some novel tweak that people in power want as opposed to harping about structural inequality for the umpteenth time." The "hamster wheel of tweaks" we are trapped on, he concludes, "not only distracts people from thinking about root causes" of crime. It perpetuates the misguided search for "the new idea that will change things without having to *change things*."

Will resurgent demands to abolish ICE—the rallying cry that first achieved national prominence during Trump's first term—ultimately meet the same fate that efforts to reform the police did in Minneapolis and around the country? As prominent Democrats call for more training for immigration officers and DHS Secretary Kristi Noem now advocates equipping federal officers with body cameras, another iteration of the cycle that Karakatsanis identifies looks to be in the offing. Together, *The Minneapolis Reckoning* and *Copaganda* suggest the outcome of democratic movements for change is highly sensitive to both the complex interplay of public demands and existing institutions in particular contexts and the news and narratives conveyed by the media.

But the brutality of Trump's war on immigrants and protesters—along with the massive and growing scale of public outrage and resistance—may be radically changing whatever calculus seemed set in stone even just a few weeks ago. The current federal assault on Minneapolis threatens to rupture the delicate rebuilding of the MPD and the fragile détente forged between the police, residents, and the city's political leadership in the years since Floyd's death. Mayor Frey, reelected once again last November, has enjoined ICE to "get the fuck out of" Minneapolis; he has also stated that he opposes abolishing the agency. This much we can say: achieving meaningful reform is sure to entail one battle after another for the foreseeable future in which public pressure, broad-based coalitions, and clear-eyed analysis of the forces at play are essential to rolling back this wide-scale state violence and abuse. **BR**

CONTRIBUTORS

Ash Ü. Bâli is the Howard M. Holtzmann Professor of Law at Yale Law School.

Benjamin Balthaser is Associate Professor of Multi-Ethnic U.S. Literature at Indiana University, South Bend. His latest book is *Citizens of the Whole World: Anti-Zionism and the Cultures of the American Jewish Left*.

Salih Basheer is a Sudanese photographer. His latest collection is *The Return*.

Adam Bonica is Professor of Political Science at Stanford University. He writes the On Data and Democracy newsletter on Substack.

Joshua Craze is writing a book for Fitzcarraldo Editions on war, violence, and bureaucracy in South Sudan. His writing has also appeared in *n+1*, *The Baffler*, and *The Guardian*, among other places.

Gerald Epstein is Professor of Economics and a founding Co-Director of the Political Economy Research Institute at the University of Massachusetts, Amherst. His latest book is *Busting the Bankers' Club: Finance for the Rest of Us*.

Vivian Gornick's most recent book is *Taking a Long Look: Essays on Culture, Literature, and Feminism in Our Time*. She received the 2026 Robert B. Silvers Prize for Literary Criticism.

Marie Gottschalk is Edmund J. Kahn Distinguished Professor of Political Science at the University of Pennsylvania. Her latest book is *Crime and No Punishment: Wealth, Power, and Violence in America*.

Jake Grumbach is Associate Professor at the Goldman School of Public Policy at the University of California, Berkeley, and a contributing editor at *Boston Review*. He is author of *Laboratories Against Democracy: How National Parties Transformed State Politics*.

Robin D. G. Kelley is Distinguished Professor and Gary B. Nash Endowed Chair of U.S. History at UCLA and a contributing editor at *Boston Review*. His many books include *Freedom Dreams: The Black Radical Imagination*.

Aziz Rana is Professor of Law and Government at Boston College. His latest book is *The Constitutional Bind: How Americans Came to Idolize a Document That Fails Them*.

Emmett Rensin is author of *The Complications: On Going Insane in America*. His writing has appeared in the *New York Times*, *The New Republic*, and *Bookforum*.

Olúfẹ́mi O. Táíwò, a columnist at *Boston Review*, is Associate Professor of Philosophy at Georgetown University. His books include *Elite Capture: How the Powerful Took Over Identity Politics (And Everything Else)*.

Liv Veazey is a journalist whose reporting has appeared in *New York Focus*, *Hell Gate*, *n+1*, and elsewhere.

David Austin Walsh, a columnist at *Boston Review*, is a historian and author of *Taking America Back: The Conservative Movement and the Far Right*.